Puddles from a Drooling Mind

…a Quest for Meaning through an Informed Faith

Denis Joseph Stemmle

Library of Congress Control Number: 2014905022

ISBN: 10:1496103998
ISBN-13:978-1496103994

DEDICATION

To Dee: the love of my life, my partner on the journey.

CONTENTS

ACKNOWLEDGMENTS

Thanks to all who invested their faith in me and this work by reading it and offering their insightful suggestions. I am especially grateful to my wife Dee, who perpetually encouraged me, but also never pulled her punches in helping me to refine this work. I also thank my brother Jim Stemmle who often stretched my mind, and Frank and Cathy Ward, Dr. Anne Dichele, and Barbara Mariconda – who all have their fingerprints all over this work.

Introduction

There must be more to life than this!

I envy faith-filled people who live in the certainty of their beliefs. I'm not one of them. I rarely accept proclamations, dogmas, pious practices, or traditions without examining them carefully. It's hard not to notice that attendance is declining in our churches — so there must be many others like me who don't see faith or morality in black and white terms. Yet I think of myself as a religious and moral person. Also frustrated and confused at times — especially when I can't seem to get satisfying answers to my questions about faith.

This is a book about my own search for meaning through an informed faith, an intelligent faith. I invite you to come along with me as I struggle with the important questions related to faith, spirituality, organized religion, and morality.

Some of the questions that trouble me:

- Does it matter if many dogmas don't seem all that important?
- Why does God make himself so obscure?
- Does God value piety? Does it really matter to him how much time I spend on my knees?

...and an even more interesting question: if these things don't really matter, then what does matter? What things should be important to a person seeking an informed faith?

And what, exactly, is an informed faith? To the best of my knowledge, there aren't any textbooks on living an informed faith. It is possible that I invented the term myself. I know that blind faith, the faith I was born into, the faith I was raised with, doesn't quite do it for me anymore. Dogmas, and what I do inside a church building, while important, are the least significant elements of faith, at least for me. If I am a faith-filled person, you should be able to see that faith clearly in what I do during the rest of my life – outside the church building. It can best be seen in how I treat people, especially those I am closest to. But an informed faith? In many ways, it is a matter of seeking out better answers than the ones packaged up for me by well meaning people who have influenced me over the years. Or at least tried to.

Frankly, I don't always do very well in reaching satisfying answers to my own questions. I just know instinctively that the questions are important, and that I should be at least trying to think them through. Sometimes I do end up at least seeing things more clearly. And I hope that you will too – or at least reach a higher level of satisfaction that comes from thinking about the right things. This book is more about taking the questions seriously than about presenting convincing answers. The satisfaction is in the journey.

I used to think of myself as a skeptic, but now a "seeker of truth" sounds a lot wiser. I have always been blessed, and often cursed with an active mind. This book will be interesting for people, like me, who normally resist pat answers, especially religious ones. And if nothing else, most religions are chocked full of pat answers. There must be more to life than pat answers.

Not everyone will be drawn into the thoughts and questions I pose in this book. For many, faith doesn't need to be all that complicated. But, others have walked away from active religion precisely because they experience a focus on ritualism and external manifestations of faith. People of great faith who actively try to convert others and bring them into their churches can be the very thing that scares away people who don't share that same great faith. Active evangelizers sometimes think of those who harbor doubts as people who need to be fixed.

I am a closet introvert – and I don't want to be fixed by someone else. As such, I am a little put off by people who are showy in their religion. In her terrific book *Quiet, The Power of Introverts in a World that Can't Stop Talking*, author Susan Cain points out that some religions are geared for extroverts. Rick Warren's Saddleback is a great example. Extroverts are drawn to the excitement of evangelical churches where the liturgies are highly entertaining and involving. Extroverts often draw energy from groups, especially enthusiastic groups like the huge congregation at Saddleback.

I practice Roman Catholicism – which I have come to think of as an introvert's religion. During my lifetime, I have worked closely with 30 or so priests – enough to get to know them personally - and I can think of only three of four of them that I would label extroverts. The rest are closet introverts like me. And the people in the pews often seem to value the solitude and anonymity that most Catholic services offer. They prefer to pray fervently but silently. People like me may enjoy exciting liturgies full of singing and interacting with those around us, but sometimes it seems like if we don't have time for reflection in our prayers, we don't come away feeling holier. I suspect that this is not so for extrovert religions. The sense of group excitement from the liturgies gives many extroverts energy and the stimulus to go out and evangelize. The questions that are important to introverts – like exactly what do I believe and why do I believe it – may not be all that important to extroverts.

So, this book may not appeal to extroverts or to people of strong faith who have never questioned what they believe. I envy them for their faith – but that is not who I am. Genuine extroverts and people whose faith is so strong that they never question the dogmas of their church are unlikely to need an informed faith. They are already informed enough – and I am happy for them that their faith gives them such satisfaction.

Nor is this book likely to appeal to people who proclaim themselves Christian, but never bothered to ask what that really means. In *A Passage to India*, E. M. Forester described one of his characters (Ronny) as a person who "approved of religion as long as it endorsed the National Anthem; but he objected when it attempted to influence his life." In my experience, this describes a good many people who call themselves Christian. And I suspect that one reason so many have walked away from their faith is because of those Christians who object when their religion tries to influence their lives. In my view, that is not Christianity at all. Faith should influence every aspect of our lives – or at least lead us to reflect on the challenges offered. Unlike John Lennon's vision in which he invites us to *Imagine* a world with no religion, I would prefer to imagine a world where people actually let their religion affect their decisions and the way they live and behave towards each other. If the two billion or so Christians on our planet all actually followed the teachings of Jesus, there would be no more hunger and no more wars. Instead, we would heed the call to feed people when they are hungry. We would respond to the call to be peacemakers and turn the other cheek and forsake revenge. No, I don't think Christianity has actually been tried very often by very many people.

Rather, this book is for the people who have hung in there trying their best to live their religion despite the fact that they may have a lot of hidden niggles that they are not comfortable talking about with other people of faith. It is also for those who have walked away from their faith because things don't quite add up for them, and for people of faith who are seeking a better understanding for relatives and friends who don't seem to share their faith. Those who have walked away have usually not given up on listening to that inner voice that drives them to make sense of things that are often called mysteries, for lack of a better term. When they believe, they want to believe in their minds as well as their hearts.

Time Magazine recently named Pope Francis as their man of the year. Reporter Nancy Gibbs stated: "At its best, (Christianity) inspires and instructs, helps and heals, and calls the faithful to heed their better angels." She later added: "a church obsessed with its own rights and righteousness could inflict more wounds than it heals." For me, that is precisely the dilemma a person seeking an informed faith faces. While it is exciting that we now have a Pope who is more focused on the core messages of Jesus, not on all the rules for sanctity that have sprung up in the 2000 years since, it still always comes back to what do I believe. How should I let my faith affect my life? This book is for people who are trying to sort out those core messages from the zillions of other messages put forth in the name of earning salvation and avoiding damnation.

Informed faith is a religion of the mind as well as the heart. Many of the faithful are delighted and perfectly content to live a religion of the heart. But for some of us, that is not enough.

For me, one of the most important elements in the search for an informed faith is taking the time to reflect. Life in my world seems to consist mostly of distractions, some of which invade uninvited, and some of which I seek out in order to cope. Time for genuine reflection gets lost in the process. And that is incredibly sad. Skimming through life, forming thoughts based on opinion polls, settling for pat answers driven home by compelling personalities and authority figures all leave me feeling a little too superficial. I was almost half way through my life before I discovered the value of reflection. It is only making the time to reflect that helps me to see what is essential and valuable and worthwhile about my journey through life – and maybe beyond. The thoughts in the following pages are the products of some of those reflections.

I lived most of my life in the world of technology. In that world, there were usually correct answers to any question or problem. It still throws me when I can't nail down a precise answer to important questions. But that, too, is part of what I mean by an informed faith. It is a matter of living with soft answers, or no answers at all. For me, that continues to be an adjustment and a challenge.

So, this book is a kind of a spiritual journey, as told through a mix of impressions, personal stories, conversations, and a sometimes fumbling attempt to sort out what is really important in the pulsating chaos that keeps presenting itself as the "real world." There are three parts of this journey: re-discovering the things that influence me, the challenges of relationships, and trying to understand who God is - the real one - and what He wants of me. These three elements are the essence of an informed faith.

Perhaps a few words about the title of this book would be in order. I associate the word "drooling" with two things: it is something geezers do, and it also connotes anticipation of something desired. Both uses of the term seem to apply to me: as a geezer, I am no longer content to let certain questions remain unaddressed. They seem to leak out of me. And in the process of applying my mind to the issues that have always baffled me, I find myself anticipating a little more satisfaction from the insights that have evolved from the effort.

How to Read this Book

I suggest three ways you might want to use this book. First, it could be simply read at whatever pace seems appropriate to you. But I would suggest that you not try to read it too quickly. If at any point something gets triggered in you – an insight, or something disturbing, or a way of thinking that is new to you – I recommend that you stop right there, close the book, and spend some time just thinking about it. Feel free to reject it, or make it your own, or come back to it later. Don't just go "Hmmm," and keep right on reading.

You could also use this book as a deliberate stimulus for your own personal reflection. I am incredibly blessed to have a life partner who has joined me in both taking the time to have, and taking the time to share our reflections with each other - daily. It's a discipline we try to practice. And we have many friends who do solo journaling. Journaling is the act of making time to just sit and think – and recording your thoughts in the process. What makes this reflecting time work for me is selecting worthwhile questions to think about. Most of my best insights about myself have come from these reflection sessions over the past thirty-five years. My hope is that whether you have a partner or not, you will use the thoughts offered in this book as another step on your own journey. My gift to you is the questions. Your gift to yourself is taking the time to reflect on your own answers. So, if you are not yet a journaling person, this could be a good time to start.

A third way to use this book is to stimulate discussions between friends. Over the years, I have been fortunate enough to be part of a number of groups of people who were on their own journeys… people interested in discovering their own distortions, and thereby seeing things more clearly. There is no substitute for the thrill of discovering a personal insight. Sometimes my own "aha moments" have been triggered by listening to somebody else's aha insights about themselves and their world. Maybe the best way to use this book is not like a typical book club might do (i.e. read the whole book and then discuss it all.) Maybe the best way would be to limit the reading and discussions to a few chapters at a time.

So, after each chapter, I offer you some questions you might use for either reflection or discussion. I should warn you though: these are not easy questions. You will probably not be able to answer them off the top of your head. They require some thought. They are targeted to people who are comfortable journaling. And if you don't like my questions, make up your own questions based on whatever gets triggered inside you. Pay attention to your niggles.

The philosophy that guides me in these writings can be summed up in the following three quotes:

> *"The truth is on some level always beautiful – and healing – to those who honestly want truth. Anything that shakes you with its 'trueness,' and anything that sucks you into its beauty does not just educate you, it transforms you!" -Richard Rohr*

> *"There is only one fault, only one: our inability to feed upon light." -Simone Weil*

> *As the fox said to the Little Prince: "What is essential is invisible to the eye."   -Antoine de Saint-Exupéry*

That is the essence of reflection: finding the truth, feeding upon light, and discovering what is essential. This is the story of my struggle to understand what is truth, light, and essential for me.

Denis Joseph Stemmle

PART 1: INFLUENCES

My most important discovery in my quest for an informed faith is the fact that I am intrinsically biased! My view of the world is warped.

I was born into a Roman Catholic family. I was taught by nuns and brothers and priests. I have practiced the Catholic faith all my life. But for the past twenty years or so, I have started asking myself why this faith is so important to me. The question I dread most is "why do you still go to church?" asked by people who have walked away from their faith. Unfortunately, I don't have a very satisfying answer to that question. And part of the reason I started writing this book was to find a personally true answer to that question.

Psychologists outline for us the principle influences in our lives. In the first four or five years, our parents almost exclusively determine our value system. In grade school, teachers, pastors, and other authority figures take on more of the role of influencing us. By our teen years, our peers affect our values the most. As our understanding of the world expands, we start the process of rebelling, or tossing out some values and embracing others. The movies and stories that resonate, and the people who become our heroes, also have a profound influence on what we end up valuing.

By the time we become adults, we have well programmed ideas on what is right and wrong, good or bad, desirable or undesirable. Our wiring is more or less complete. By this time, we have all the distorted vision we need. We have a way of seeing and coloring and filtering the happenings in our own world in certain familiar and comfortable ways – and we tend to dismiss or reject those who interpret things differently.

*It took me a very long time to admit to myself that what I was taught and came to accept as a kid could actually be a biased, distorted or filtered way of looking at my world and interpreting it. I struggle to accept the fact that I am a composite of paradigms created by my own history. I see the world **not as it is, but as I am**. However, I don't believe that all truth is relative. Part of the quest for an informed faith is understanding the difference between my truths and the real truths. Discovering absolute truths is not an easy task.*

This first section addresses the people who have influenced the way I think, interpret, and see my world.

I. The Song My Dad Sang to Me

Most of the programming, biases, distortions, and filters baked into me as I grew up were really good for me. But every now and then, something happens to me as an adult that causes me to change the way I see my world. Here is one example.

My Dad passed away about eight years ago. He worked hard most of his life at the Post Office, and he never had a lot to say. I was the middle one of his five kids.

Mom once told me that Dad thought I should have been a salesman. He never mentioned it to me directly. I assume he thought I would be a good salesman just because, as a kid, I did not have a problem walking up to people coming out of church - and asking if they wanted to buy a raffle ticket on a car. The nuns challenged us to do that, and I guess I was one of the few who actually rose to the challenge. I won a lot of holy cards for my efforts – then I didn't know what to do with them. (They kept falling out of my prayer books.) I might have been a successful salesman. It just never occurred to me. And Dad never mentioned it.

Instead, I became an engineer. And I was good at it. I never had a problem with math, algebra, trig, calculus, etc. And as soon as I graduated, I took a job in another city 600 miles away from my parents. My wife and I soon had four kids of our own, and were up to our ears with my career, and doing church work and community service. Some days, life just seemed to be whizzing past me. Before long, it was rare to see my Dad more than twice a year – usually at Christmas, and maybe once during the summer.

Dad never really sang to me (as the title implies), and he rarely said anything directly to me beyond the pleasantries. I don't think he liked the fact that my life was so busy – and we lived so far away. But, with one exception, he never gave me any advice, and I never asked him for any.

The one exception is something that stuck with me all my life. It may be one of the reasons I am writing this book. What he actually said was sort of a platitude. But coming from Dad, it meant a lot to me. I now try to think of it in more dramatic terms. I imagine my Dad as Danny Kaye in the movie *Hans Christian Anderson*, and I am a thirty-five year-old little kid sitting at his feet as he points out an inchworm in a flower garden.

Dad has a slight frown on his face, and he sings just like Danny Kaye did:

> Inchworm,
> Inchworm.
> Measuring the marigolds.
> You and your arithmetic, you'll probably go far.

(A tear starts rolling down Dad's cheek. He continues in a

whisper:)

> Denie,
> Denie.
> Measuring the marigolds.
> Seems to me you'd stop and see
> How beautiful they are!

I have always had a problem letting beauty actually sink in. Dad probably did too. For me, appreciation is sometimes a painful process. I struggle with allowing myself to appreciate the beauty around me, whether it was marigolds or people or ideas. I have to set aside my mind and acknowledge my soul… and that has never come naturally to me. And whenever I allow myself to be struck by inherent beauty of something right in front of me, I want to grab onto it and hold it – and probably destroy it in the process.

So the key words in what I imagine my Dad singing to me, what makes all the difference to me, are the words "stop and see." That, I can choose to do.

And what does all this have to do with finding meaning through an informed faith? I believe that Dad's advice is probably the most important element of developing an informed faith. If I never "stop and see," my world will remain very confined and limiting. An informed faith is neither confining or limiting.

Questions for Reflection and Discussion:

-What are some of the marigolds in my life that I should spend more time seeing "how beautiful they are?"

-John Lennon famously said "Life is what happens while you're making other plans." What are some aspects of my life that I think I may be failing to appreciate?

II. Advice that Changed my Life

Most of the advice I have been given over the years has been unsolicited. And very little of it actually registered with me. But there are some notable exceptions. The first chapter was about a piece of advice that my Dad gave me. I would not say that one changed my life. It is more accurate to say that I am still processing it, still making myself "stop and see," and still struggling to appreciate the beauty that is right in front of me.

But, there were three occasions when the advice I received had such an impact on me that my life changed dramatically because of them! These are worth sharing. And it only occurred to me much later that each of these pieces of advice was, in fact, an important element in finding meaning through an informed faith. They all boil down to this question: **Whose yardstick am I going to use to judge what is of value in <u>my</u> life?**

Brother Antonio:

Brother Antonio was my physics teacher in my junior year at St. Xavier High School in Louisville. He might have been a newly minted Brother… I really don't know. What I do remember is that he came to us from the Bronx, where he had spent all his life up to that point. And it was my first experience of somebody from New Yauwk. He talked funny… saying things like "youse guys." For some reason, he thought the plural possessive of "you-all" was "youse guyses." It took us smart asses from Louisville most of the year to straighten him out. Anybody from Louisville knows that "you-all" is actually a singular term. The plural of "you-all" is "yer-all". And the correct plural possessive of "you-all" is "yer-allses," as in "take out yer-allses physics books now." But whenever we succeeded in getting Brother Antonio to say it properly, it sounded about as funny as when he said "youse guyses."

My junior year was when I started getting serious about my relationship with Dee, who later became my wife. Dee and I would take the city bus to school together, get off five or six blocks early, and walk the rest of the way – hand-in-hand. She went to an all-girls school a few blocks past St. X, my all-boys school. Brother Antonio used to tease me about Dee. He'd greet me with "I saw you squiring that young lady again this morning…" and then he would mimic the two of us walking down the sidewalk. I didn't know I was squiring her, but I guess I was.

Anyhow, one day late in the school year, Brother Antonio asked me after class "So, what are you going to study in college?" I told him that I was thinking about becoming an engineer. He thought for a minute and said: "OK, but don't be a dumb one." I wasn't quite sure what he meant by that, since I didn't actually know any engineers at that point in my life. I must have had a quizzical look on my face. So, he clarified it for me: "Most engineers are fairly intelligent when they're talking about engineering stuff. But if you try to get them on a different subject, they usually don't have much to say."

Very interesting. I think it was his New Yauwk way of advising me to get a real education, not just career training. It was based on this exchange that I decided to get a degree in Liberal Arts before going to engineering school. As a 17 year old, it was probably the smartest decision I ever made.

Brother Antonio, in his Bronxian sort of way, provided me with a second element to developing an informed faith. Too much focus on material success puts blinders on me. Such a focus is guaranteed to squeeze out any ability to ask and ponder on the more important questions in life. When career dominates my life, what I "stop and see" remains a very narrow slice of the real world.

Chuck Gallagher:

In 1974, I made a big discovery on a Marriage Encounter weekend: that I was a lousy listener. I started to come to grips with the fact that I was a defensive listener. I listened for opportunities to jump into the conversation and make my points. I listened with a focus on how I could respond in ways that made me look and sound intelligent. When I listened to Dee, my focus was not on her, it was on myself. Big insight!

So, after that Weekend, I started trying my best to practice active listening to Dee – paraphrase what I thought she was trying to say, feed it back to her, test for understanding, seek clarification, etc. I worked hard on improving my listening skills. And I thought I was turning myself into a pretty good listener.

Chuck Gallagher was a Jesuit priest who singlehandedly turned Marriage Encounter into a major renewal movement. He had a reputation for demanding a lot from the people who worked with him. He hated qualified answers to his requests. He would confront people with "Tell me you will, or tell me you won't. But don't tell me you can't!"

Chuck had a real gift for cutting through the crap, and calling husbands and wives to greater intimacy with each other. One time, I was telling Chuck about my progress in becoming a better listener. He responded by asking me if Dee felt listened to? To which I replied "What?" Chuck looked me right in the eyes and said: "It doesn't matter one bit how good of a listener you think you are. The only thing that matters is - does she feel listened to?"

Chuck's advice was another turning point in my life. It didn't take me too long to realize that his advice applies to nearly everything in my relationship with Dee. I discovered on my own that the same advice applies to the way I love her. It doesn't matter how much I think I love her. All that ever matters is how much she feels loved.

Chuck's gift to me was another key element to developing an informed faith. If I am not living out every detail of what I claim to believe in my relationships with the people I am closest to, then my faith and religion counts for nothing the worst sort of hypocrite.

George Simpson:

Chuck Gallagher also introduced me to the concept of re-evaluation. He emphasized that we each have much more control over our lives than we imagine. When we find ourselves in life-draining situations, it is important to recognize that we have the power to change it. Most of us continue to live lives of quiet desperation by making default decisions. When we do nothing to change a situation that's sucking the life out of us, that's a decision by default.

After about ten years working at a large technology company, I found myself moving up the management ladder, and taking on more and more responsibilities. At one point, I realized that I was in way over my head. I had responsibility to lead a group of about 40 engineers and scientists on a high priority product development program. I was working six and a half day weeks, and usually 12 to 14 hour days, and bringing work home every night. This went on for months on end. My wife and kids were becoming strangers, and I wasn't handling the stress very well. I growled a lot. The kids would say "Hi Daddy" when I walked in the door, and I would just want to bop them and tell them to get out of my way. I didn't, but that's what I felt like. I hated being an absentee father and an absentee husband. And I hated how the stress was leaking out of me.

It was the first time in my life when I felt the need to re-evaluate the decisions I had made that got me into that situation in the first place. I knew I wanted to get out of that job, and get back to a more balanced life. The problem was this: my current boss went way out of his way to get me promoted into that position – years before most people rise to that level. And most of my peers would have traded their firstborn child, or their left testicle, to be in the position I had. And if I walked away from that job, it would probably turn into a black mark on my personnel record – and affect the rest of my career at that company. Not to mention disappoint my boss – who had helped turn me into a rising star.

On the other hand, it was a big enough company that I knew I could find dozens of interesting jobs, probably all involving demotions. I didn't mind the prospect of a demotion – but I wasn't sure what the ramifications would be for my future.

I agonized over this decision for weeks, not knowing what to do. Other than Dee, I didn't know who I could talk to about my dilemma. She suggested that I talk with George Simpson, a previous boss, who was one of the few people in that company who had a capacity to listen. George had recently come back to work after surgery for some kind of cancer.

I went to see George. I explained that I wanted to change jobs, but I was worried about the prices I would pay. It would be a slap in the face of my boss, who had leveraged a lot of political capital to get me into the job I wanted to leave. I would be abandoning my team at a critical point on the program. I would end up with black marks on my records, and who knows how such a move would affect my future prospects. But I was paying big prices by staying in the job – and my wife and kids were paying even bigger prices.

George listened patiently to me. He seemed to understand the dilemma. When I was done pouring out my exasperation, he said: "I have just two questions for you to ponder. First, what's the worst thing that could happen?" I didn't need to think much about that one. I blurted out: "I could get fired!" Then George said: "Question two: if that actually happened, could you handle it?" I replied: "In truth, it would be a big relief." The economy was good enough that I knew I could easily get another job somewhere. So, George looked at me and said – "So, what's the problem again?"

And I realized he was right. The next day, I walked into my boss' office and requested a transfer. My boss was disappointed in me, but he approved it. I didn't get fired. And I became a better husband and father – at least for a while – as a result.

Since then, I've frequently found myself in equivalent situations – needing to step back and re-evaluate, or maybe just fretting over something I wasn't quite sure how to deal with. George Simpson's advice never left me. Those two questions are pure magic when I am facing a difficult decision: What's the worst thing that could happen? And, if it did, could I handle it? My answers to those questions have given me the courage to walk away from overly stressful jobs five or six times. And maybe even more importantly, calm myself down when what I am fretting about isn't really all that important. I have a way to see that now.

George provided me with yet another key element of finding meaning through an informed faith. It is so easy to cope, accommodate, absorb, and just suck up those elements of my life that create such stress that I blind myself to what is really important. George's message was this: if your journey takes you down a path that is eating you up, walk away. Take another path.

So, I owe a lot to Brother Antonio, Chuck Gallagher, and George Simpson,– each of who cared enough about me to change my life with their wisdom. While they never heard the concept of an informed faith, they each offered me insights into important truths. But they didn't become my truths until I acted on them.

Questions for Reflection and Discussion:

-What are some conflicting priorities that lead to stress in my life? How do I handle these? Are there actions I should be taking instead of living with the stress?

-What are some pieces of advice that have affected my life?

III. Searching for Truth

*The key phrase from Dad's advice was "stop and see." It turns out that acknowledging my own soul is a lot harder than it sounds. I bury it below a lot of crap and self justification. Finding the truth in any situation requires me to throw up a big time-out signal - and take the time to see – and think. Think about what? One of those questions that I rarely hear anybody asking any more is the Pontius Pilate question: **What is the truth?** In college, I was taught that discovering underlying truths was an essential part of education. Once I lost my idealism, I discovered that there are a lot of barriers to discovering the truth.*

Righteousness is one of them. Righteousness makes it nearly impossible to "stop and see." And because of all the distortions in the way I see and interpret my world, I am most blind to my own righteousness. And that righteousness makes me blind to many other things.

Righteousness has no place in an informed faith. In fact, it prevents it.

And most of the people who influenced me over the years were righteous people, usually in the best sense of the word. But, maybe it just seems that way because I have only recently come to see the dark side of righteousness.

First, some pronouncements: The problem with righteous people is that they think they are right! I often have a hard time with such people, even though I need to count myself among them. People who are actually willing to spend time in reflection are rare birds in our world. Righteous people almost never take the time to reflect. But man-o-man, it's really hard to see your own righteousness, and let go of it – if you never reflect on it. It's way easier to see it in others.

I am righteous whenever I am so convinced of the correctness of my own opinions that I refuse to consider any alternatives. Righteousness replaces the search for truth. I am righteous whenever I know what is true without ever questioning it. Righteous people don't want understanding – we'd rather have labels. We are label factories – as if the whole truth is contained in the label. "You're a (fill in the blank) – and that's all I need to know about you!"

A good place to see flagrant righteousness in action is in political debates. It can be very entertaining when candidates act like pit bulls tearing into each other. They see no need to consider what the opponent has to say, except to prepare a rebuttal. Most political debates are simply a matter of trying to get the labels to stick to the opponents. The righteous people we elect to Congress are against each other's opinion even before they hear it. They legislate by sticking their fingers in their ears and saying "Na, na, na, na, na…" until the person from the other faction finally shuts up. Reflection and listening are becoming lost arts. In fact, the most awful thing a politician can say about an opponent is that they changed their mind sometime in the past… as if careful reflection is a character flaw.

Yet, I hate to admit it to myself, but the above stereotype of a political debate is often how I behave in the middle of arguments with my wife. But I have great difficulty seeing the righteousness in my own behavior.

I have often heard it said that most of the worst atrocities in the history of human existence have been perpetrated under the banner of religion. I submit that the real cause of most atrocities is not religious differences at all. It is righteousness. And label slapping! The labels give us all we need to know: Zionist, Refugee, Islamist, Terrorist, Enemy, Tea Party, Liberal. We are all saying God is on our side. But God cringes every time we say it.

Jesus railed against righteousness, and the ruling authorities did away with him. Righteousness killed Ghandi, and Martin Luther King, and John Kennedy, and Abraham Lincoln. Their killers were so filled with their own righteous convictions that they could justify any action.

I have been working on trying to see my righteousness more clearly. I would love to get myself to the point where I don't have a righteous bone in my body. But every now and then, I discover the truth. For example, when I re-read the last three paragraphs, which could come across as a righteous screed, I start to see how intolerant I am - of intolerance. That's just another form of righteousness.

Recently, I caught myself indulging in righteous indignation. My sister, who lives 1000 miles away sent a chatty e-mail, and her last line included the statement: "I have breast cancer. I don't want to talk about it. If you want to get the scoop of what is going on, talk to my daughter." I wrote her back immediately and asked her for more details. She replied by again referring me to her daughter. I sent the daughter an e-mail, and didn't hear back for a week.

I mentally excoriated my sister and her daughter for their lack of communication skills, and I found myself getting highly irritated over her making it so difficult to find out some simple facts about what was going on. For a week, I fumed in my own righteous indignation. I did nothing. I just stewed.

During one of my daily reflections, it finally occurred to me that my righteous indignation is still righteousness. I started to see how I was acting childish. Pouting. Instead of focusing on their behavior, I should have been asking myself "what else might be going on here?" So, after not hearing anything for another week, I called my sister's daughter, and found out that my sister has stage-four breast cancer that has spread to her bones. After consulting with three medical friends and researching this further, I reached the conclusion that she may not have very long to live. Had I continued stewing in my righteousness, I would never have discovered the truth about her condition.

On a personal level, I also discovered a truth about myself. Righteousness only hurts the righteous! I can see this in the way I react to our adult kids when I think they are not listening to me. It usually means that I am not listening to them either. And any time I find myself in a righteous argument with my wife, I not only stop listening, I sometimes even stop being civil. So long as I remain smug in my righteousness, I don't even know that I am hurting myself — much less the people I care about. I need to rediscover the art of asking myself questions I would rather not have to think about. Like: am I being righteous, and is that a barrier right now?

With respect to finding meaning through an informed faith, this constitutes another important principle: Righteousness left unchecked is a barrier to insight. And compassion. Righteousness, even in the best religious sense of the word, is usually thinly disguised bias, bigotry, and superior attitudes.

Questions for Reflection and Discussion:

-What are some ways I have engaged in righteous indignation? How might I be hurting myself when I do that?

-What kinds of things make me indignant? How might that be blocking my ability or my desire to see the truth?

IV.When I Don't Like "Their" Answers

If I am determined to rebel against righteousness, especially in myself, then **what do I hang onto after I start questioning pat answers**? *Once I start to doubt conventional wisdom, it can be bewildering. Some of the most important questions are the ones I don't want to think about, until someone rubs my nose in them.*

In his homily three weeks before Christmas, Fr. Lynch asked, "Why do we need a savior?" It was such a great question that I shut down and didn't hear the rest of the homily. The first thought that popped into my head was all the troubling discussions we've had in the parish recently about why 80% of the people who are members never come to Mass – except perhaps to celebrate the birth of our Savior – and maybe His resurrection. I thought Fr. Lynch's question was a much better question than why don't they come to mass? Maybe it is exactly the same question. If they knew why they needed a savior, maybe they would come to church more often.

But shutting down during the homily was my typical way of dealing with a disturbing question that I needed to ponder. Maybe I shouldn't be thinking about *them*, I should be thinking about *me*! And I didn't like the fact that I didn't have an answer to that question for myself. Why do *I* need a savior?

Actually, my life is pretty good! I am retired. My wife and I have enough money to pay the bills, live in a fine home, go to plays and concerts when we feel like it, and travel around a lot. None of our kids or grandchildren are in jail, and they're all more or less healthy. I try to live my faith, and I try to be generous to the people in need around me. What do I need to be saved from?

About 30 years ago, a young man named Wayne just returned from what was a life-changing experience for him. He found Jesus. He cornered me, full of righteousness, and asked me if I have accepted Jesus Christ as my personal savior? I told him that I have been a lifelong Catholic, and I have never walked away from the Church. Wayne persisted: "But have you accepted Jesus as your personal savior? If you can't name the time and place when you accepted Jesus as your personal savior, then you haven't been saved!" He was literally thumping my chest with his finger as he said this.

I was offended by what I perceived as his 'righteousness.' In fact, this event with Wayne probably led me to write the previous chapter. Righteous religious people come across to me as fanatics - with a superior attitude... "I've got my Jesus – here, let me ram him down your throat!" In fact, a part of me suspects that the problem with those 80% of our parish that don't come to mass is that they, too, have big problems with righteous people.

As I sat there not listening the rest of the homily that morning, I thought about Wayne, and I finally asked myself if maybe Wayne was just asking me a question I didn't want to think about. Like, "Why do I need a savior?" and "What is he saving me from?"

For the past ten years or so, I have been reading everything I could get my hands on to try to learn more about who was the real Jesus and what did he actually mean by all that he preached. Instinctively, I know that there is something wrong and distorted in many of the messages our churches are putting forth. I frequently drive past an incredible church facility that has over twenty thousand attendees every Sunday. I call it "Six Flags over Jesus." The message they preach is "Jesus wants you to be well off." I don't think so. And there is the other extreme – the fundamentalists. Much of what is put forward in the name of religion and righteousness seems to be simple intolerance for anyone who considers different answers from what they think Jesus meant. So, for the past ten years, I have been searching for what did Jesus actually say, and what did he mean? I don't really think he wants me to be rich, and I don't think he wants me to be narrow minded. But that's not too helpful – because it is limited to what I shouldn't be, and how I shouldn't think. What is the positive side?

Maybe I just don't want to think about his real message. I can get very defensive over "sell all you own and come follow me." (Maybe I could start with the bowling ball. Haven't bowled much anyhow.) Why should I try to be meek when God didn't make me meek. He gave me a good brain and many opportunities to use it and make important things happen. What does it mean to be poor in spirit? And what is he saving me from? I wish I had a good answer for that one.

Maybe the answers aren't in the answers. Maybe the answers are in the questions! Maybe what he came to save me from are pat answers – one size fits all kind of thinking that come from the Waynes, the Six Flags over Jesus, and the fundamentalists of the world – and all the others who are determined to push unsolicited advice on me in the form of what just seems like platitudes. Jesus constantly had to confront a wall of Pharisees who had all the answers that he knew were not only too pat, but often harmful to people. And there were times when He seemed unsure of himself – and also had doubts about things – like "Abba, why do I have to go through this?" Maybe saving me is simply a matter of planting some great questions in me, and letting me wrestle with them in my own way. Maybe when He said "follow me" so many times, what he meant was this: ask questions the way He did. He was born into a pretty awful world, yet spent his life challenging the way things were while preaching about the way they ought to be. In a world that claimed holiness is found in following the formulas, He taught that holiness is found in forgiveness and compassion and in loving each other – the greatest commandment.

Maybe I am *supposed to* shut down during the sermon – and actually reflect – on where am I not being forgiving or compassionate or loving. Maybe my salvation lies in the questions, in the uncertainty, in the reflection. Maybe that is the best I can hope to do. Search.

That seems to be yet another aspect of finding meaning through an informed faith. Faith is way more than simply living by the rules. Sometimes, like Jesus, faith is a matter of questioning the rules – or at least understanding the important principles behind the rules. An informed faith is built on questioning and searching.

Questions for Reflection and Discussion:

-What are some important questions where I have trouble accepting answers based on conventional wisdom? Why am I troubled by them? What are some of the things I do in order to either live with or ignore my own uncertainties?

-What are some things about religion (my religion?) that don't ring true to me?

Denis Joseph Stemmle

Part 2: Relationships

Only a small part of the search for an informed faith has to do with what happens while I am on my knees. While reflection, insights, discoveries and beliefs are all very important starting points, an informed faith has more to do with how I live out what I profess to believe. And the real test of my faith is how I interact with the people I am closest to. My faith is occasionally evidenced on the street.

Most often, though, it is evidenced behind closed doors. That is the hardest place to live out my faith - with the people who know me best. This section is about that struggle.

V. Whatever Happened to Sin?

*My Church gives out a lot of unsolicited advice –
except she doesn't call it advice. She calls it homilies,
and Canon Law, and papal edicts. Much of it is good,
but like all unsolicited advice, I find it easy to either
ignore or dismiss with "why is this important in the first
place?" Some of it doesn't seem very important at all.*
**Does a person seeking an informed faith need to
embrace everything that is taught by persons in
positions of authority?** *I am not going to attempt to
answer that question here. But it is an important
question to me.*

*At the start of Advent in 2011, the Catholic Church
decided to change many of the words of the English
version of the Mass so that they would more
accurately reflect the "original Latin" version of the
Mass – which I assumed meant the version many of
the clergy grew up with before Vatican II. Original for
them, I guess. That led me to wonder about how
important using the right words is to God – and I*

concluded that He probably didn't care very much.

*But that doesn't mean to imply that using the right words is unimportant – especially outside of the church building. When the Church changed the words, it led me on a convoluted path toward personalizing the question into **"How do my words lead me to sin these days?"** That is probably an important element of living an informed faith.*

Early 2012: I did it again this morning! The priest at Mass said: "The Lord be with you." And I rattled off "and also with you." Most of the people around me answered correctly ("and with your spirit") because they were looking at the handy cards in their pews to help us all get the words right. But one or two of those people looked a little sheepish like me, as we started searching for cards in our pews. The next time the priest said "The Lord be with you," I heard a voice behind me just answer: "whatever!" Most of the people around me giggled at that. On the way home, I found myself wondering if the words are all that important. Isn't the essence of our spirituality found in how we act, and not in what we say?

Well, maybe it's in both. But this question is worth me taking the time to reflect: how can my words lead me to holiness, or into sin? Sometimes how I act out my faith **is** found in the words – and not just at Mass. Often my spirituality, and sometimes my lack of spirituality is evident in what I say, and when I say it, and how I say it.

For some reason, while driving home from Mass that morning, I found myself thinking about my favorite scene from the film *Elmer Gantry*. Elmer was a travelling salesman in the days before there was a television in every hotel room. He was an agnostic, but he spent a lot of time reading Gideon Bibles – mostly because there wasn't much else to do in the evenings. He became fascinated by the "religion business," as he put it. At one point in the movie, he found himself at the pulpit in a tent revival meeting, ready to give a sermon. Elmer is standing at the pulpit, gripping it with one hand, Bible in the other hand, sweating a little, hair a little disheveled, staring out at the congregation, who are waiting eagerly for him to speak.

And he says: **"Sin, sin, sin! You're all sinners! You're all *doomed* to Perdition! You're all going to the stinking, scalding, everlasting stench of a painful hell!!!** ... (long pause.) **...Unless you have love."**

I love that quote. I used to do a pretty fair impersonation of Elmer Gantry doing that sermon at parties when I was a teen. But, even today, that scene resonates with me – mostly because it reminds me of what I grew up hearing from the pulpit. The sermons my pastor delivered in my youth were right out of *Elmer Gantry* - about sin and damnation. And it occurred to me that I just don't hear much about sin any more. Has sin become obsolete? Has it been replaced with "whatever" - as the voice in the pew behind me said that morning? Has our religion gotten so easy that we're never supposed to feel bad about anything anymore?

Maybe one of the real benefits of slightly changing the words at Mass is that I now have to pay attention to what I am saying. In time, I will probably get over it, and get back to the point where I can just blurt out the correct responses on auto pilot again. But for at least a little while, I am paying attention to the words. And guess what?! Elmer Gantry's message is right there in the words of the Mass: "I confess … that I have **greatly sinned** - in my thoughts, in my words, in what I have done, and in what I have failed to do!" Sin is not obsolete! We just don't talk about it anymore.

I no longer buy the whole Elmer Gantry routine – especially the parts about Perdition and hell. But, I do buy the beginning and the end bits: "we're all sinners…unless we have love." I believe sin exists, but I don't think my sins are found on the lists of sins I remember memorizing for the nuns in grade school. As a child, I didn't want to go to hell, so I had to make sure that I didn't steal, murder, cheat, or "distobey" my parents. Now, as a married man, it sometimes seems an even bigger challenge to accept that I am sinning whenever I renege on my solemn oath to love, honor, and cherish my wife, Dee. When I break a sacred promise, what else would you call that but sin?

That's what that prayer at Mass says to me now: I can sin by failing to love - in my thoughts (about Dee), in my words (to her), in what I have done (to her), and perhaps most importantly – in what I fail to do (for her.) To live up to my wedding promises, it is a constant challenge to find ways to love Dee the way she needs to be loved, not necessarily the way I am most comfortable doing the loving. I have to let go of who I'd prefer her to be. When I don't do this, I sin "in what I fail to do."

My failures to love are usually not out in the open for all to see. They're hidden. I sin whenever I start thinking of myself as a victim or martyr – which I don't want anybody to see because it looks weak and wimpy. I also sin whenever I mentally reject, or just tolerate Dee's strengths, all the while wishing she would change to be more like me. I sin whenever I let my cranky feelings turn into cranky words with critical overtones. I sin against Dee whenever I remain pulled back and cautious because I'm secretly blaming her for something instead of taking responsibility for it myself. Whenever I let a distance between us go on for days at a time, knowing I can mend the relationship any time I want, I am choosing to violate my sacred oath. I didn't promise to love, honor, and cherish as long as I feel loved, honored, and cherished myself. I promised to love proactively. It's just a question of integrity: did I mean what I promised or not?

Elmer Gantry was right: "we're all sinners… unless we have love." And part of having love is acknowledging culpability and seeking forgiveness. So, what I started doing is adding a few words of my own to the new words of penitential act at Mass. This prayer starts out: "I confess to Almighty God and to you, my brothers and sisters…" It's not at all clear to me how I sin against the "brothers and sisters" around me at Mass. So what, exactly am I asking forgiveness for? Yet, with Dee, I can think of a lot of things I need her to forgive. So, instead of saying "my brothers and sisters," I am now saying "I confess to almighty God, and to **you, Dee**, that I have greatly sinned – in my thoughts, in my words, in what I have done, and in what I have failed to do."

That way, I remind myself that I still take my wedding promises seriously. Informed faith requires way more than discovering new insights and seeking objective truths. Sometimes the hardest truths to discover are in my own behavior, and how that affects the people I love.

Questions for Reflection and Discussion:

-What are some of the ways that I sin against those that are closest to me?

- (For married people): How do I live out my wedding vows today – in my thoughts, in my words, in what I do, and in what I fail to do?

-(For unmarried) Do I think of my failures and my mistakes as sins? What constitutes sin for me today?

VI. The Prairie Chicken

Sin, for a person with an informed faith, takes many forms – especially in intimate relationships! Too often, my focus is on what I get out of the relationships rather than what I invest in them.

The "Strengthfinders" books by the Gallup organization are built around the key point that each of us has native strengths, and life satisfaction comes from using these strengths to be who we were designed to be rather than focusing on what we or others think we ought to be. This is a hard lesson to absorb in our world.

*The best intimate relationships comprise people who are consistent in celebrating each other's strengths – who fully accept each other for who they really are. The important question I am wrestling with in this chapter is **"How can I get better at celebrating the people around me for who they are, rather than who I wish they were?"***

Father Bill Dilgen passed away last year. He was a good friend. He had a remarkable ability to listen, and ask just the right questions. Plus, he was filled with curiosity, highly intelligent, well read on most subjects, and truly enjoyable to be around.

Fr. Bill once delivered a sermon that affected me more than any other sermon I have ever heard. Most Biblical scholars agree that of all the sayings in the Gospels attributed to Jesus, the parables are the most likely to be true to what Jesus actually said. And with few exceptions, he didn't try to interpret the meaning for his listeners.

Fr. Bill's memorable sermon was a simple parable. He was probably not the originator – I am sure he read it himself somewhere. And I have re-told it so many times, who knows how close my memory of the story is to the original. But, in any case, this is what I remember of Fr. Bill's sermon that day:

A young boy was climbing a mountain one morning, when he came across an eagle's nest with eggs in it. He rejoiced to himself, saying "I have always wanted to have an eagle of my own. I can take one of these eggs home with me, hatch it, and I will have my own eagle." So he carefully picked up one of the eggs, climbed back down the mountain, and took it home with him.

Later that day, he showed the egg to his father and told him about his plans to raise the eagle. The father placed his hand on the boy's shoulder and said:

"Son, you cannot keep an eagle. Eagles were meant to be free, to soar high in the heavens, and to live the way God intended them to live. So you take that egg back to the nest where it belongs. Let the eagle be free."

The boy was sad, but he knew it was no use arguing with his father. So, he set out late that afternoon for the mountain. Along the way, he came across another nest with eggs in it. This was the nest of a prairie chicken. The boy was getting tired, so he thought to himself: "If I put the eagle egg in this nest, then I won't have to climb the mountain again. Plus, birds can't count – so the prairie hen will hatch this egg along with the others. Then, the eagle will be free, as it was meant to be."

So, that's what he did. And he went home believing he did the right thing.

And sure enough, when the prairie hen came back to her nest, she did not notice that she had an extra egg, and it was quite a bit larger than the rest. She simply hatched all the eggs – as she was meant to do. And then she set about teaching her new brood of chicks how to fend for themselves.

The prairie hen knew that her chicks needed to learn how to feed themselves. So, she taught them how to scratch in the dirt to find good bugs to eat. She taught them how to recognize danger, and then flap their little wings while they were running away so that they could run faster. She knew that eventually, they would actually learn to fly a few feet off the ground as a faster way to escape danger.

The little eaglet learned all these lessons along with all his brothers and sisters. As he grew bigger, he noticed that he didn't quite look like the rest of them, but they seemed to accept him as he was – and that was fine with him. Besides, he learned to be very good at feeding himself and escaping danger like a good prairie chicken.

One sunny day when the eaglet was out with his brothers and sisters - scratching in the dirt and finding bugs to eat - he happened to look up. He noticed a magnificent bird soaring in the sky above him – and it took his breath away. He was transfixed at the sight of such beauty and majesty. "Wow," he said out loud to no one in particular, "Isn't that incredible!" None of his brothers or sisters bothered to look up to see what was there. They were too busy scratching in the dirt. So, the little eaglet persisted: "Hey" he shouted, "would you look at that! Isn't that the most beautiful sight you have ever seen? I wish I could do that!"

One of his brothers finally glanced up in the sky and said: "Oh, that's an eagle. You could never soar like that. You're just a prairie chicken."

The brother went back to the business of finding bugs to eat, and the little eaglet soon joined him.

And the little eaglet lived all his life, and then died, thinking he was a prairie chicken!

At this point, Fr. Bill just sat down next to the altar for five minutes. He didn't interpret the parable for us... he just let us have time to reflect on it. Then he got up and resumed celebrating the mass.

I strongly recommend that you stop reading right now, and close this book for five minutes. Use the time to reflect on this parable for yourself. Then I will share with you what I thought about for the five minutes.

OK, welcome back. I heard Fr. Bill's sermon over thirty years ago. It sticks in my memory because it led me to a very important insight about myself. It was a troubling time for me. I had been dwelling on yet another story that disturbed me a lot. This one was "The Man of La Mancha," the Broadway play about Don Quixote. If you are not familiar with that play, the plot revolves around a sickly old man who was losing his mind. It was the time of the Spanish Inquisition, one of the uglier periods in the history of the human race – and all of the people around Don Quixote had lost hope. Chivalry had been dead for two hundred years, but Don Quixote loved to read romantic novels about the age of chivalry. And soon he found himself transformed into a "knight errant," out to right the wrongs in the world. As he put it, "I intend to bring a measure of grace into this world."

In his adventures, Don Quixote came across a self described "kitchen slut" named Aldonza. Aldonza was a tough woman out of necessity. She worked as a scullery maid at an inn that catered to the lowest form of humanity. When mule skinners and the like stayed at the inn and had gotten themselves drunk on the cheap offerings at the inn, they often paid Aldonza for sexual services, which she did willingly but with disgust.

Don Quixote didn't see that facility as an inn - he saw a castle. And the skuzzy proprietor of the inn was the Lord of the castle in Don Quixote's mind. And Aldonza was not a kitchen slut to him, she was the beautiful Lady Dulcinea. He treated her as a lady, and she didn't know quite how to handle that. As she put it: "Blows and abuse I can take and give back again. Tenderness I cannot bear." Yet, despite her rejection, Don Quixote persisted in treating her as a lady – and she found herself wanting to believe his version of her. Nobody had ever treated her like a lady before.

As the play progresses, Don Quixote gets himself in a lot of trouble. His relatives succeed in bringing him back to reality in order to sign some documents handing his assets over to them when he died. And eventually Don Quixote finds himself on his deathbed, a broken and confused old man. The ugliness of reality has beaten him. It is the Lady Dulcinea who comes to him as he is dying, and says "Please, try to remember. You looked at me and you called me by another name." And, barely audibly, Don Quixote says to her: "The words…. Tell me the words." And Dulcinea sings to him his own words in the song "The Impossible Dream." …"to fight the unbeatable foe, to bear with unbearable sorrow, to run where the brave dare not go… to be willing to march into hell for a heavenly cause. And I know if I'll only be true to this glorious quest, that my heart will lie peaceful and calm when I'm laid to my rest. And the world will be better for this… that one man, torn and covered with scars, still strove with his last ounce of courage, to reach the unreachable star."

In the process of singing his own words to him, Dulcinea transforms Don Quixote back into the knight errant he knows himself to be. He gets up out of his deathbed and prepares to go off to right more wrongs. And he dies while putting his armor back on.

To me, this is another story of transformation... transformation in the opposite direction from the way the eaglet was transformed into the prairie chicken. Don Quixote transformed Aldonza into the beautiful Lady Dulcinea. And in the process, she becomes strong enough to return the favor, and transform him back into the visionary he was meant to be.

Why did this play have such an impact on me? It started me thinking about my relationship with my wife, Dee. Somehow, I knew that I needed to see the Lady Dulcinea in Dee, and help her to see it in herself. I needed to be a visionary who saw the good in her, reflected it back to her, and celebrated the beauty in her that she couldn't see in herself. But the reality was, while I had been thinking about this a lot, I wasn't making much progress in this quest. She remained suspicious of my motives, and defensive sometimes.

And then I heard Fr. Bill's sermon. And in that five minutes when he sat down after relating the parable, I stumbled on a very troubling insight. Most of us have had people who loved us also tell us that we're just a prairie chicken in one form or another. But, more importantly, I recognized for the first time that I have the power within me to influence how the people around me see themselves – and I can guide that transformation in either direction! In all of my relationships: with Dee, with our kids, with my brothers and sister, with our parents, and with my co-workers and friends - how I phrase what I say to them influences how they see themselves. My words have power – to raise up, or to tear down.

While I had been hoping to transform Dee into Lady Dulcinea by affirming the good I saw in her, it had never occurred to me how often I said the equivalent of "you could never do that… you're just a prairie chicken" to her – and thereby undermined my own efforts. How much was I limiting her? Had I created the Aldonza in her? Or at least a part of it – along with every other person that was important in her life? Every time I was critical of what I saw as her shortcomings, no matter how subtly or artfully I tried to disguise it, wasn't I just tearing down her self-image and making her defensive? All the times I have taken her for granted, and failed to be grateful for all that she brought to our relationship, wasn't I not much better than the mule skinners in the way they treated Aldonza. In what ways had I made her feel used? It turns out that that is a very difficult, but also a very important question to spend time reflecting on. For example, all my married life, clean socks and underwear magically appeared in my drawers, and the house was clean, and meals were on time – as if the fairies did that while Dee was off holding down a full time teaching job, not to mention a full time parenting job for our four kids. How often did I even acknowledge her decisions to love in all that consistent effort? Instead, I found myself saying things like "I wish you would learn how to swim, or use the remotes, or the computer, or get yourself into better shape."

Fr. Bill's parable helped me to see that if I wanted to help create Lady Dulcinea, I had to *stop* creating Aldonza! I had been trying to transform Dee into someone she was not, instead of cherishing and celebrating her for who she was.

All her life, people had been telling her "you're just a prairie chicken," including me. My new quest was to see her for what she was – a loving woman with a beautiful soul. And I needed to teach myself how to celebrate that. With gratitude.

So, what does all this have to do with finding meaning through an informed faith? Its pretty simple. The best evidence of living an informed faith is not just seen in how I treat the people I am closest to - but more importantly, in how I celebrate them for who they are.

Questions for Reflection and Discussion:

-What are some of the ways I say the equivalent of "you're just a prairie chicken" to the people who are important to me?

-What are some steps I could take to learn to celebrate more consistently the people who are important to me?

VII: Twilight Time

For a person with an informed faith, nothing is ever perfect. Whenever I find myself stewing about the things that are not as perfect as I would like, I often end up losing sight of what is important. Steven Covey makes a great distinction between things that are urgent and things that are important. When there are too many urgencies in my life, I have great difficulty remaining aware of what is truly important. I end up giving away my days with no real return. I fail to "stop and see."

And I am getting too old for that.

*The important question that I need to keep reflecting on is this one: **How should I be investing the time that remains in my life?** The following story only gives a partial answer to that question – but it also emphasizes just how important it is to be asking myself that question in the first place.*

(This story seems to work better when I tell it in the third person; but I am the character Don in the story. And my wife is the character Deb.)

There seemed to be two of him in the room. Two Dons. But he wasn't sure. In the background, he might have heard soft music playing – but he wasn't sure about that either. It could have been Deb in the other room, playing the music from the oldies station again. But then, wasn't she watching a basketball game? Maybe the soft music could have been just a tune running through his mind. Yet he heard it distinctly – the old Platters song:

Heavenly shades of night are falling, its twilight time.

Out of the mist your voice is calling, its twilight time…

One of the Dons was in a dark corner of the room, leaning against the hutch with all the decorative plates Deb had collected over the years, just staring out into the room with no expression at all on his face. The other Don was sitting by the window, likewise just staring out without much expression. Well, maybe there was some expression… his eyes were quite red.

The Don by the window seemed absorbed in watching the rain trickle down the pane. It never seemed to take a straight path. Sometimes the little streams would take an abrupt right for no apparent reason – then start moving down the pane again. There wasn't much light left in the day, so Don just sat and watched it fade away. Most of the time, his eyes were looking out at the cold rain, but his mind wasn't seeing it. His mind kept drifting off into other places.

One of those places was seeing his own hands. For years, he had had hints of essential tremor – where his fingers would tremble for no apparent reason. It didn't bother him much, except when he was trying to read the paper. Sometimes it was hard to focus on the paper when it was shaking in his hand. The tremors were more of an embarrassment than a problem. Deb never seemed to mind except when they were sitting doing crossword puzzles together, and she couldn't read the clues because the paper was shaking.

But five days ago, he noticed that the tremors were so much worse. He remembered watching his hands, as if they were not his own hands, trembling as they brushed the raindrops off Deb's casket. They had just finished the final prayers, and they were about to lower her into the ground. But there were all those raindrops on the casket – and that would never do. He had to wipe the raindrops off the casket – except his hands were shaking a little too much to be very effective at it. Then one of his adult daughters stepped in and started wiping off the raindrops with him. And then the other three of their kids started helping. And then the grandkids helped. Don found himself wondering, now, why that was so important to him then. He didn't know why. It just was.

Other images started to take over the window. The rivulets of rain faded away, and in their place was a refrigerator full of casseroles. So many casseroles. After five days of eating casseroles, he couldn't remember what any of them tasted like - yet the refrigerator was still full of them. At least now, people have stopped bringing more casseroles.

All the people have left and gone on with their own lives. They all seemed to say the same thing: "Are you going to be OK?" as they said their good-byes. And Don assured them that he would be OK.

Now he was at the window, and it was raining, and he thought he was OK. There was something therapeutic about watching the little rivulets zig-zag down the window. And the window kept turning into sort of a screen with images he couldn't seem to control: him trying to feed baby food to Deb last month as she lay in the bed with the covers pulled up around her chin. She didn't really want the baby food, and could barely swallow it – yet somehow she managed to smile at him. And then they were dancing: Don in his tuxedo and Deb in her flowing gown, waltzing to Annie Murray singing "May I have this dance, for the rest of my life? Will you be my partner, every night?" They were singing the words to each other. And then Deb was quite youthful and naked in front of him, and his fingers softly trailed down her side – making little goose bumps in their path. And then the two of them were just walking hand in hand – a country walk in springtime - just happy to be with each other.

Don slowly turned away from the window with a vacant gaze, and looked into the room. And there she was. Or at least it might have been her. She was a little hazy, and had a bluish tint all about her. But she was smiling at him.

"Hi, Kiddo," he said.

"Hi, Stud," she replied.

"I miss you," he said.

"I'm not really gone," she said.

"You've been to the other side?"

"You know I can't answer any of your questions. You

will just have to wait and see for yourself."

"What do I do now?" he asked.

"You'll be OK."

Don watched her as she faded into the darkness of the room. "Everybody thinks I'm going to be OK," he thought.

Now what? He didn't want to think about 'now what.' It was just easier to sit for a while and watch it rain and grow darker. He didn't even know what he wanted to do after he got up out of the chair. Now what, indeed.

He'd think about that later. He had a long time ahead to think about it.

The other Don remained standing in the dark corner leaning against the hutch, watching the first Don as he glanced down from the window and seemed to notice for the first time that his hands were shaking. The first Don heard that melody again: *"Out of the mist your voice is calling..."* – and this time, he was convinced that it existed only inside his head.

As he stared across the room, the second Don slowly faded away until there was nobody sitting at the window. And just as slowly, the sounds from elsewhere in the house seemed to creep back into his consciousness. It sounded like a basketball game on TV. Then he heard Deb shouting at the TV – "Oh NO!"

Don walked into the TV room, and Deb said "Siva just blew a three pointer, and then Giang got the rebound, but he stepped out of bounds with it, and there's only eight seconds left!" Don loved to watch Deb watching basketball. He loved to watch her shouting at the TV. It was one of the joys of his life. And so what if the team blew another one.

It took another four minutes for the eight seconds to pass. Then Don took the remote and turned off the TV, took Deb's face in his hands, and quietly kissed her and stroked her cheek. Deb wasn't quite sure what brought that on – but she liked it when he stroked her cheek.

Author's note: a person seeking an informed faith does not give away days fretting about things that are urgent but not important.

Questions for Reflection and Discussion:

-What is it about the way I am spending the time I have left that I am not sure is the best choice for me?

-Imagine an important person in your life passing away. What would be your regrets relative to your relationship with that person?

Part 3: Evolving Faith

Now we get to the "faith" part of developing an informed faith.

Living my faith in the ways I treat the people that are part of my life is, in many ways, the easier part. It involves a lot of reflection and self examination, and frankly my motivation to make my relationships as good as I can is fairly pragmatic. I want to live a satisfying and fulfilling life. The state of my relationships affects 90% of what leads to satisfaction and fulfillment – or sometimes leads away from these things. While the values of investing in my relationships spring from my faith, the benefits have little to do with faith. It is just a pursuit of happiness thing.

For me, the more difficult part is what, exactly, do I

believe about the nature of God, and Jesus, and all the "truths" my church teaches? There are so many ways to approach these questions. One way is simply to believe what people tell me. But my mind gets in the way. Do I really want to believe in a God who is capable of condemning his creatures to burn in hell for all eternity if they don't live up to a set of standards? Why would God be so sadistic? It just doesn't make sense to me – and thankfully my church seems to have backed away from teaching about this sort of God. So, if God is not sadistic, then what is He?

A number of years ago, I decided to go to the source. I decided to read the Bible from cover to cover, attend five or six years of bible study classes, then read everything I could get my hands on to see what the Biblical scholars and religious thinkers had to say about what is written in the Bible. Authors like Marcus Borg, Bart Ehrman, John Dominic Crossan, Raymond Brown, NT Wright, Gary Wills, Elias Charcour, Joan Chittister, and Richard Rohr now fill many bookshelves in my home. I read some of the documents from Vatican II. I also had the opportunity to travel extensively and experience cultures outside my own little world. And - oddly for an engineer, I guess – I started to read the classics I never had any inclination to read in my formative years…things like Homer's Iliad, Dante's Inferno, Plato's Republic, etc. So, as you will see in the coming chapters, I started drawing comparisons in the process of trying to ferret out the truth – and determine what to believe.

Much of what I read was so ponderous that it took a

lot of self discipline to get through it. And as a result, I didn't want this next section to be a dry exposition on the nature of God and the Church. So, in places, I decided to have a little fun with it all – while still trying to make important points. Buried in the next chapters are the products of a serious search for a fuller understanding of God and my Church.

Of course, I didn't succeed in this quest. So, read these chapters as a snapshot of where I am so far in my journey. Many of my doubts remain intact. But the quest for meaning through an informed faith is based on the following quote:

"Who never doubted, never believed.

Where doubt is, there truth is.

It is in her shadow."

-Gamaliel Bailey, American abolitionist (1807 – 1859)

VIII.   A Competition for My Soul

*Here is an important question I need to ask myself on
the way to finding meaning through an informed faith:*
**if I had not been born into a Christian family,
would I choose Christianity for my religion?** *I
have noticed that for much of the world, what you
were born into determines your religion. Most
Europeans and Americans are Christian, most
Middle-Easterners are Islamic, and most Asians are
Buddhists. It is easiest to just stick with what you
know, and what most people around you profess to
believe. The vast majority of "believers" seem to do
just that. But, in the spirit of discovering an important
truth, what would happen if we could take away the
element of culture. Would any particular faith make*

more sense than any other?

One method for finding truth, meaning, and developing an informed faith is by conducting "thought experiments" when it is not possible to conduct real experiments. For example, a question most people try to deal with sometime during their lives is "what happens after I die?" Most of us were taught about going to heaven, or paradise, or some other good place as a reward for living a good life. Yet, there is no evidence whatsoever that there is even an afterlife, much less a heaven. There is just no way to confirm anybody's beliefs on this. So, let's do a little thought experiment.

Let's suppose that all my life, I had been marooned on a tropical island. My parents were tragically killed by some natural event when I was quite young. So I grew up in a Garden of Eden – all alone. I had everything I needed: plenty of natural food, warm weather, a cave to shelter me during the occasional storms. I lived in paradise. I spent my days gazing out at the sea that stretched to the horizon all around me, wondering about the meaning of life. Who am I, why am I here, and what happens to me after I die? When I was still a child, I absorbed knowledge about relationships by watching my parents interact with me and each other. But, I grew up not knowing how to read or write, having never been exposed to either eastern or western literature, or religion, or politics. I was a blank slate, with a curious mind. And usually bored. I had reasoned my way to the conclusion that there must be at least one supreme being of some sort who had created my paradise. But that's about as much religion as I could generate for myself.

So far, pretty cool, huh? But every good story needs some dramatic event to disturb the tranquility. So, here's the dramatic event. One day, three missionaries made their way to my island. They all wanted to save my soul, which I didn't know I had. They didn't appear to like each other very much. They were always arguing with each other and shouting each other down. They certainly disturbed my tranquility, but I found them all quite fascinating. Not boring. And they all wanted to teach me about their Gods and their faiths.

Eventually, in order to absorb what they were all trying to say, I had to send two of them to the other side of the island so I could sit and listen to them one at a time.

Missionary A started by telling me about his faith. He mentioned that the real world outside my island was teeming with other people, and that's why the world needed his religion. Religion helps people get along with each other. He believed there was only one God, who watched over the people who embraced this faith he was telling me about. His God was mostly benevolent, but He didn't care much for people who did not accept this faith. His God wanted his people to do good and avoid evil. I wasn't sure what "good and evil" actually meant. So he explained that doing good involved tithing 10% of everything you owned every year, and giving it to people in need. Avoiding evil mostly meant self denial and not eating the wrong kinds of food, and avoiding any action that caused harm to another believer. For example, fornicating with a woman you were not married to was an evil – and God dealt harshly with people who despoiled virgins.

I told him that my parents were killed many years ago by a natural disaster. I asked him where they went after they died? And where would I go? He said that my father was in Paradise and was rewarded with 70 virgins to despoil at his leisure. He didn't know where my mother went.

Wow! Despoiling virgins sounded like a great way to spend eternity. That would solve my problem with boredom. There weren't any virgins on my island. But, being a bit of a smartass, I asked him why, if despoiling virgins was an evil when you were alive, how come you were rewarded in heaven with the chance to despoil 70 virgins – and it is not evil then?

He didn't have an answer for that. Nor did he know what happened to women after they die – but it didn't matter, since I was not a woman.

Parts of his religion made a lot of sense to me, and part of it didn't make any sense at all. So I sent him back to the other side of the island and asked for Missionary B.

Missionary B started by telling me about his faith. He too mentioned that the real world outside my island was teeming with other people, and that's why the world needed his religion. He wasn't too sure how many gods there were, but it didn't matter. His religion was concerned with living a good and moral life, getting along with others, and with achieving tranquility in the process. His religion seemed to focus on the soul. Since I already had more tranquility than I knew what to do with, I wasn't sure that I followed his logic. I asked what happened to people after they die? That was becoming the most important question to me. He told me that forty days after you die, you come back as another person, and you are given another chance to achieve serenity and tranquility in your lifetime. If you don't quite make it, then after you die again, you come back again and again until you finally get it right. I asked him what keeps people from achieving tranquility? He said it was mostly other people who were to blame. So, I asked what happens when you finally figure out how to live a tranquil life, and then you die? He said that that has only happened to one person that he knows about, and that person became sort of a god.

Hmmm. Maybe my life on this tropical island means that I finally learned how to achieve tranquility in all my previous lives – and here I am as a reward. I must already be a god. Tranquil, but bored. I noted that there were no virgins to despoil with this guy's version of the truth. One virgin would be nice, but maybe that would screw up my tranquility in the end. While I liked tranquility, I would also like some excitement in my afterlife.

Missionary C also believed in one God just like Missionary A, and also mentioned that the real world outside my island was teeming with other people, and that's why the world needed his religion. That was becoming a familiar theme. The God of Missionary C had a cruel streak. He sent his only son to be tortured to death as a way to atone for the sins of all the people. As a result, if I were to believe in this God and lived a moral life, when I died, I would be rewarded with the privilege of gazing on the face of this God for all eternity. I asked if Missionary C had ever seen this God, and he said nobody has. I asked what if He's a really ugly dude – why would I want to spend all eternity gazing at him? He said, trust me, you'll like it.

OK, so there's the issue: which one of these versions of the afterlife make the most sense? Despoiling virgins, tranquil but bored, or gazing on the face of somebody I have never seen before - for all eternity. Actually, none of them sound all that appealing. And I suspect that all these "truths" are just made up. Nobody really knows what happens after we die – so they all speculate on it. Maybe we just die, and that's it.

The reality is, most of the teachings of the principal faiths in our world have similar ideas about morality and how to live a good life. They all have different "sacred mysteries" as answers to things that cannot be figured out. But they all provide some kind of an answer to that longing in our souls that keeps us searching for God – and searching for meaning in our existence here on earth. So that part is good.

I recently read a book by a young lady who interviewed hundreds of people about their ideas on what will they find in heaven. She could discover no trends in their answers, except that heaven involves something that is missing in my life right now. (That's probably where the 70 virgins idea came from.) That may be my problem in a nutshell… nothing important is missing in my life. I am pretty happy where I am.

No, wait. I want better answers, and I can't find them. Maybe heaven is where I will find the truth. A person seeking meaning though an informed faith will never find all the answers in this lifetime. Maybe that's all heaven is. Answers! And truth!

Questions for Reflection and Discussion:

-What do I think heaven will be like for me?

-Spirituality is a matter of "letting your soul seek God." What are some of the ways that my religion enables this?

IX: The Evolving God

When I think about evolution, most of the time I think about it in the past tense, as if it is now all completed. Of course it isn't. We are still evolving… and who knows what we will eventually evolve into.

God seems to be evolving too. My religion teaches that there is one true God. I find myself wondering which one is the true one? He seems to have changed a lot over the centuries. There have been times on my spiritual searching when I just wanted to shout "Will the real God please stand up! Why are you being so damned obscure?"

Things used to be a lot simpler before I started asking questions. When the nuns were teaching me, there was no ambiguity. Good was good, bad was bad, and God was God. And if you screwed up, you got punished. And we are the One True Church. I was brought up to believe, like a fundamentalist, that the Bible was the inspired word of God – and that every word came from Him. Every word was the Truth.

I thought of faith as a static thing – that what is proclaimed now has always been proclaimed in the same way. But, our belief systems seem to keep changing. I started noticing many similarities between what the Bible says and what other religions once believed, and I found myself wondering if the Bible simply records a series of "beliefs-du-jour". The next couple of chapters include many stories of many "truths" and many gods. They all attempt to address the questions: **Does my faith have a corner on the truth? And what, exactly, is the Bible?**

Vindictive Gods:

In the ancient days, I doubt that theologians from different religions ever sat down with each other and engaged in theological debates. Communication channels around the world weren't so good, so they probably didn't even know about the diversity of religions and belief systems across the world. Yet, despite this, there seems to be a lot of commonality in the way they interacted with their gods.

Imagine an ancient Incan priest – let's call him Sam - in a theological debate with a Jewish Patriarch… say, Isaac. They both existed in roughly the same time frame, about

3500 years ago.   Sam is clean shaven, muscular, mostly naked, has stripes of paint all over his face and chest, and random feathers sticking out all over the place. Isaac is lean and weary looking, wears a simple tunic made out of a burlap bag, and sports an impressive black beard. They are seated on two stone benches under a shade tree.

Sam admits he doesn't know exactly how many gods there are, but he's pretty sure that there are more than one. And Isaac is absolutely certain that there is only one, but he can't disclose his name. Sam asks "why not?" Isaac replies "because I would be dead if I said his name out loud." Sam asks "Are you sure?" Isaac admits that he doesn't know of anybody who ever tried to say God's name out loud, but he's pretty sure nobody has ever risked it. Sam allows as to how some of his gods are also prone to doing such silly things – like not wanting people to know too much about them.

Anyhow, Sam thinks that it is a ridiculous idea to worship only one god, and Isaac thinks the Incan is a primitive who has his head stuck up his ass – feathers and all. And the two could argue – nose to nose – for hours on the number of gods there are. But, fortunately they eventually get around to asking each other about their relationships with those gods. And there, they start to find some common ground.

> Isaac: So how do you worship your gods?

> Sam: Our gods constantly need to be appeased. They are prone to anger and likely to commit atrocities on my tribe unless we frequently acknowledge our subservience. Just last week, one of the gods went a little crazy and started tossing

lightning bolts around – and actually killed a fellow priest who was standing on the top of a pyramid at the time – begging the god to calm down a little. The gods go crazy all the time.

Isaac: No shit? How do you appease them?

Sam: Human sacrifice, mostly. Our people built really impressive altars in the shape of huge pyramids. We go up on top and sacrifice virgins and enemies and other random folks by ripping their hearts out and holding them up for the gods to see.

Isaac: And that works?

Sam: Well, I have recently started to wonder if this is such a good idea, especially when one of the gods is going crazy and the risk is higher for being struck down by lightening. We're losing too many good priests when the gods get angry. So, our Incan tribal council decided that we need to conduct the human sacrifices only in good weather – and hopefully appease the gods *before* they go crazy. It's sort of a preventive maintenance strategy.

Doesn't your God go a little crazy every now and then?

Isaac: I suppose he is often displeased with us. Our minds tend to drift.

Sam: So, what do you do to appease Him?

Isaac: I almost didn't survive past my eighth birthday because my father was about to sacrifice **me** – his only son – to appease the One True God… for some reason or other. Being a child at the time, I never quite caught the reason why my father would sacrifice his only son.

Sam: You sacrifice your own kids? Don't you have any virgins around? And how come you're still alive?

Isaac: Well, I found out later that our God likes to test his people to see if we are still loyal to him. His way of going crazy is to lapse into fits of jealousy, lest we start to worship other gods. Which, admittedly, we are prone to do every now and then. Anyhow, apparently God sent his angel to my father to stop him from sacrificing me. The angel more or less said – "kill something else."

Sam: Lucky you.

Isaac: From that point, our Hebrews tribe started debating what the angel was trying to tell us. Was it permission to stop the human sacrifice? Or was it just this once – because I was such a special kid, or something? Nobody seemed to know.

The more they talked, the more Sam and Isaac became amazed that there were so many similarities between the ways they interacted with their deities. Despite the fact that they lived on two different continents, with two different ideas on how many gods there were – both tribes needed to interact with those gods in more or less the same ways. Appease them, or pay the price. God(s) get angry or jealous or crazy otherwise.

Interactive gods:

Eventually, all the great religions of the world move on. Over time, the really progressive Incans, and the really progressive Hebrews, figured out that the gods/God would be just as appeased if they substituted killing something else – like their best bull – and saved the virgins and firstborn for other purposes. And it wasn't just the Hebrews and the Incans that moved on. Other noteworthy religions moved on too.

So let's scroll forward about five hundred years for our second theological debate. Imagine a similar conversation between another Hebrew – let's say one of the guys that wrote about the prophets of the Jewish scriptures. How about the son of Jeremiah? Let's call him Jerry Jr. And the other debater was one of his contemporaries from Greece – say one of the students of Plato. Let's call him Hesius. No, that sounds too Roman. How about Glaucon. He was a character in Plato's Republic.

Both are in their mid twenties, and both have the bloom and curiosity of youth on their sides. Jerry wears the same old burlap bag that was in fashion at the time for the Hebrews. And Glaucon is wearing a long white robe – rather elegant looking for a student. They are ambling through the agora, and seem to have all the time in the world.

> Glaucon: Tell me, Jerry, How many gods do you have?"

> Jerry: One, but I can't tell you his name.

> Glaucon: Well, we sure got you beat there. Homer listed at least 40 gods in our pantheon. The big guy is Zeus. And of course, his wife Hera…

> Jerry: Wait a minute, your best god is married?

> Glaucon: Not very happily. I'm sure he thinks of it as

a big mistake.

Jerry: I wonder if our God is married? He never talks to me – but he talks to my Dad. I'll have to ask him to ask God if he's married.

Glaucon: I sure hope he isn't. We get more troubles than we need because Zeus and Hera are always plotting against each other. And they take it out on us.

Jerry: Do any of your gods talk to you?

Glaucon: Not to me personally. But Homer told lots of stories about the gods interfering with the affairs of the human race. If they didn't come in person, they sent messengers, or omens, or appeared as clouds. They were always taking sides. And they couldn't agree with each other on much of anything. When we were invading Troy, some of the gods were on our side and some were on the other side, and if we or the Trojans ever forgot to offer sacrifices to the gods, they would often get pissed off at us and switch sides. But the short answer is yeah – they were always talking with us. And they were always roiling up the sea or causing earthquakes or changing the weather – or throwing thunderbolts to influence the outcome of whatever we were doing.

How about your God. Does he talk with you?

Jerry: Not me. But he talked with my Dad. And there were a dozen or so other prophets that had routine conversations with him. Mostly, he seemed disappointed in our tribe. We have this covenant thing. We're supposed to stay loyal to Him. But, we never seem to get it right. There is something about having just one God that most of us find limiting. So, we lapse into worshiping Baal, or some of the other gods of our neighbors. Then God talks to our prophets, and they warn us to repent and get back to honoring our half of the covenant. And most of the time, we either ignore the prophets or kill them. Then God gets pissed off and makes something bad happen. More or less like you just described about the Greeks and their gods.

So, Jerry and Glaucon started discovering a lot of things that their religions have in common. Their deities were constantly interfering in their human affairs. Their deities were demanding. They need to be obeyed and appeased and constantly sacrificed to – or they get offended.

They found the similarities quite intriguing, and started searching for other things they have in common.

Glaucon: If you think there is only one God, how do you know when he's on your side?

Jerry: He just is, that's all. Back in the days when Moses was leading us out of Egypt, we didn't think the Pharaoh had a very good god to go up against ours. Our God killed all their firstborn. It was like the reverse of the old days when we had to kill our own firstborn to appease God. Now he kills our enemy's firstborn instead. Anyhow, the Pharaoh's god was this huge stone bird – and he didn't do anything. Just sat there with a sour expression on his face. Poor Pharaoh knelt before that stone bird holding his dead firstborn son for four days and nights – and the bird just stared at him and did nothing. So, the Pharaoh let our tribe go free, then changed his mind and was chasing after us – and our God came to our rescue. He drowned the entire Pharaoh's army to protect us. What a God we got! Too bad the Egyptians didn't believe in Him too.

Glaucon: That sounds a lot like what our gods do for us. When they are on our side, they do all sort of evil things to our enemies.

Jerry: Do your gods want you to mortify yourselves to appease them?

Glaucon: Well, Priam spent four days sprinkling himself with ashes and wearing sack-cloth instead of his royal robes, in order to persuade Apollo to go to the Achilles and talk him into giving the Trojans back the dead body of Hector, whom Achilles killed. You following this? Apparently the sackcloth and ashes worked because Apollo did go talk with Achilles and persuaded him to give the body back.

Jerry: Really? We're always doing stuff like that – sackcloth and ashes – to show our God that we're sorry for screwing up again, and to persuade Him to change his mind on something.

Glaucon: When you were talking about the Pharaoh's stone bird god, it occurred to me that our gods often appear in the form of birds. Real ones. In fact, Homer talked about Zeus flying over the battlefields in the form of an eagle. Both sides took it as an omen that Zeus was on their side. I think Zeus just wanted to see what was going on down there.

Jerry: Our God shows up as a bird pretty often too.

In fact, just last month, God visited my father in the form of a raven – to bring him something to eat. We're not sure it was really God. It could have just been a messenger from God. Or maybe just an empathetic raven. But Dad was convinced that the raven was God looking out for him.

So, the more they talked, the more amazed they were at just how many similarities there were in their relationships with their deities. Their gods seemed to all act the same: direct discussions between the gods and the humans, the deities actively interfering in the lives of their subjects, appeasement, animal sacrifices, sackcloth and ashes, gods that are always scheming, or getting enraged and jealous because of what humans do, gods appearing as birds of various types…. It's like somebody wrote the script, and the two nations simply inserted their different deities as characters in the play. Is this the real picture of our One True God? I hope not. I don't like this one very much.

Despite the amicable nature of the previous two theological discussions, over the centuries, there certainly has been a lot of "my-god-is-the-good-guy-and-your-god-is-the-bad-guy" going on. We're still doing it. I astonished my co-workers once when I overheard an engineer with a turban on his head muttering "Allah be praised!" when he got some good test results. I responded "Amen, Brother!" One of my fundamentalist Christian friends overheard this exchange, and took me to task for it: "How could you endorse that rag-head's religion?" I responded: "Allah is my God too, I just call him by a different name."

Since I was brought up to believe that we are all God's

creatures and He loves us all, I found myself wondering how God could have committed the kind of atrocities against the Egyptians that Jerry described in the above conversation with Glaucon. Here is my conclusion: It was either an erroneous interpretation of the true nature of God, or it was just bad staff work. The following is a story of how that might have happened if it was just bad staff work. This version of the story should probably be included in the next update of the Bible:

Cue the Frogs

The chair at the head of the board room table was empty. The staff sat fidgeting around the table as they cautiously watched Almighty God pacing back and forth behind the chair, with a deep frown creases etched in his forehead.

> Almighty God: Tell me what planet we're talking about again?

A staffer pressed the button that scrolled the screen down from the ceiling, then pressed another button to project a map of the universe onto the screen. He then extracted a laser pointer from his pocket and pointed it toward a dot on the map. "This one. They call it Earth."

> AG: Ah, yes. That's the one where our chosen ones got themselves enslaved, Right? And why are we talking about this now?

> Marketing VP: Our latest data indicates that 93% of them have been bombarding us with requests to get them out of slavery. The other 7% are fairly content staying put. The only problem is that the 93% are

losing heart. Some of them are starting to pray to the Egyptian gods for help.

Legal VP: And we signed a covenant with them. We are obligated to respond to their requests.

AG: Refresh my memory. What does the covenant say?

Legal VP *(pulling a file out of his briefcase):* Here's the troublesome clause. It says 'I will make a covenant with the people of Israel. In their presence I will do great things such as have never been done anywhere on earth among any of the nations. All the people will see what great things I, the Lord, can do, because I am going to do awesome things for you.' It goes on in that vein for another several pages.

AG: And why did we do that covenant with them?

Marketing Guy: We were losing market share. The other gods were getting a larger piece of the pie. We had to do something, or you would have become just a footnote in the history of Earth.

AG: OK, OK. So, we wooed them with a covenant. What has our competition done in response?

Marketing VP: Not much. Their pantheon isn't very good, but they don't need to be. The Egyptians have all the power. They enslaved our chosen group, who have been bellyaching at us ever since.

AG: OK. So, what have we done about this problem so far?

Tech VP: We had Aaron turn his staff into a snake.

So, the Pharaoh's guys turned their staffs into snakes too. Then, we had our snake eat their snakes – but the Pharaoh wasn't very impressed. So then we had Moses turn the river into blood - all the while, begging the Pharaoh to let the people go free. Pharaoh wasn't very impressed with that either.

AG: *(frowning even deeper)* And that was supposed to win over the other side? And why did we think snakes and blood would be awesome – like we promised in the covenant? In fact, why did we think that snakes and blood would persuade the Pharaoh to upend his entire economy?

The staff around the table all looked down at the papers in front of them and offered no response.

AG: *(continuing to pace):* OK, what else have you come up with.

Marketing VP: Our team has been brainstorming this issue for two days. We have concluded that we need to up the ante. We think we should send a plague next.

AG: A plague is going to win over the Pharaoh?

Marketing VP: Something really awesome might.

AG: OK, what have you got?

Marketing VP: Frogs.

AG: Frogs?

Marketing VP: Frickin' frogs, Big Guy. That will be

awesome!

AG: What is so awesome about frogs?

Marketing VP: Our demographic studies show us that ninety-nine out of every hundred Egyptians have never seen a frog before. They live in the driest place on the planet. Frogs will be awesome!

AG: Your logic escapes me. How are the awesome frogs going to persuade the Pharaoh to let a hundred thousand slaves just walk away. I don't see the connection.

Marketing VP: He will be so overwhelmed by your awesome power that he will give up his stupid gods, especially that big stone bird that he thinks rules the universe, and come over to our side.

AG: That's the best you can do? Frogs?

At this point, the Marketing VP had no answer. For a full minute, the entire conference room sat frozen in silence. The Big Guy wasn't buying it. Almighty God kept pacing back and forth, just looking at the floor. Then:

AG: So, what's Plan B?

Marketing VP: We have a whole series of plagues lined up in case the frogs don't do it.

AG: Let me guess. A plague of parakeets?

Marketing VP: No, next comes gnats, then flies, then we'll kill off all their animals, then boils, then hail, then locusts – we have quite a comprehensive program lined up.

AG: Right. I can just see the Pharaoh now... "Oh God of the Hebrews, we'll trade you one hundred thousand slaves for some flyswatters." Does anybody here have any sane ideas?

IT VP: I'll take this one. Here's what we're working on, AG. Our team is about to release the Beta version of "AG in Action!!!" We've been training a teen-ager to use it, and he's getting very good at it. And he hasn't been playing all that long.

AG: Let me talk with the kid.

IT VP steps out of the board room, and returns with a skinny teen ager with acne and a sullen expression. The kid doesn't look at anybody, and just slumps into a chair in the back of the board room.

AG: I hear you're getting pretty good at using the software.

Kid: I'm already up to level three.

AG: OK, tell me about levels one and two.

Kid: They are totally awesome. In level one, we kill off all the firstborn of the Egyptians. There's blood everywhere. Then in level two we drown the entire Egyptian army in the Red Sea. Way cool.

IT VP: And in the final release version, what the kid does on the console actually happens on planet Earth. It is some of our best work!

AG: And we think that is going to increase our market share? We think that the Egyptians are going to convert to our side because we wipe out all their babies and soldiers?

A long stony silence ensued.

> Marketing VP: We need a decision big guy. They're losing their faith in you.

The long stony silence continued. AG kept on pacing with all eyes glued to him. Finally he let out a huge sigh:

> AG: OK, cue the frogs.

OK, so I went a little whimsical on you with these three stories. But, there was a serious intent behind it all. As I mentioned in the preamble to this chapter: these stories all attempt to address the questions: *Is there such a thing as absolute truth? And does the Bible record it?*

Sometimes God is a supreme disappointment to me. While most sermons I hear these days talk of God as just wanting to love us - and that kind of God is certainly more palatable than the God of the Hebrew Scriptures – I wonder if I would actually prefer the obsolete God of domination and control. That is certainly a lot less of an ambiguous God.

Questions for reflection and discussion:

-What do I think God expects of me? Why do I think that?

-If I thought of the Bible as a record of human interpretation of God rather than as the inspired word of God, how might that affect my faith?

X: Sequel: Son of Evolving God

Since I was a little playful with the Old Testament in that last chapter, I thought it would be only fair to be playful with the New Testament in this chapter. The question is the same one: **Is there such a thing as absolute truth? And does the Bible record it?** *Is what we read in the New Testament the inspired word of God, or is it a recording of how the people at the time experienced God, and his Son?*

This chapter is actually a somewhat whimsical distillation of the thoughts of the biblical scholars I mentioned in the introduction to this section – with a number of my own thoughts and observations thrown in for good measure.

For a person seeking meaning though an informed faith, the God of the Old Testament is easy to dismiss with "that's just how they saw Him back then." So, we focus on the God of the New Testament. But how accurate is this representation of God?

We're in the control room of a TV studio, looking over the shoulders of a dozen technicians sitting in front of a bank of switches and dials and knobs. There are dozens of screens in front of us, and on one of those screens is a news anchor named Ted. Ted has scored a ratings coup by hosting a panel discussion with the four Evangelists: Matthew, Mark, Luke, and John. Maybe there was some kind of a time machine involved in Ted's pulling this off – I don't really know. And it's not important.

Ted looks and sounds a lot like Ted Koppel - and I would have said that he *is* Ted Koppel, except that I haven't asked Ted Koppel's permission to use him as a character. So, he's just Ted. (Hopefully, that will keep the lawyers happy.)

There is a lot of excitement in the control room as the broadcast begins. Ted looks quite snappy in his dark suit and tie, his well coifed head, and his sincere and trustworthy way of looking directly into the camera. The faces of the four guests are seen on other screens. Matthew is also dressed in a business suit and tie, and seems quite alert and animated. He has long, black, curly hair spilling out from below his skullcap, and tassels poking out from below his suit coat. Mark is wearing the classical burlap bag, and seems quite young for an evangelist. He too sports curly black hair. Luke has that classic Greek look with his well trimmed, glorious grey beard, a serious look of contemplation, and wearing the long white robe favored by Greek scholars. John looks a bit like a hippie who has messed with the 'shrooms a little too often. His blue jeans have rips at the knees, and he looks comfortable in his tie-died tee-shirt. He tends to stare off into space a lot, and the others are not quite sure if he is really there or not. They are all sitting behind a polished wood table in the studio.

The occasion for the panel discussion is that John, the last of one to complete his Gospel, just finished the last chapter and has sent out the manuscript for his followers to review.

A few minutes before the broadcast is to begin, Ted walks around the table and introduces himself to his guests, and chats a bit with each of them. Then, the lights come up, the director counts down the last ten seconds, a technician flips a switch, and Ted begins:

> Ted: Good Evening. We are here tonight for a special event that is unprecedented in the history of religion. We have the four writers of the gospels of the Christian Scriptures – all together in the same room at the same time. A few minutes ago, when I was chatting with these guys, it was clear that they had never met each other before. In fact, they are not even contemporaries. Mark died about 50 years before John started writing his gospel. And all four of them came from communities that were widely separated from each other in both time and space.

So, let's meet the Four Evangelists!

The director gives cryptic commands to the technicians to focus in on the face of each evangelist as Ted introduces them to his unseen audience. They each looked a little bewildered as their faces appeared on the screens. After the introductions, Ted continues:

> Ted: They have each published a life story about the same man – Jesus of Nazareth. Yet, none of them actually knew him, saw him, heard him speak, or even knew any of his followers. So, we get four very different pictures of this Jesus. Mark, the first one to complete his story, describes Jesus as an itinerant preacher who travels from town to town – and gets himself into trouble a lot. For example, Mark included in his story a little vignette about Jesus boating across the Sea of Galilee and commanding a whole legion of evil spirits to depart from a man and enter a herd of two thousand pigs. The pigs promptly jumped into the sea and drowned, and the pig farmer was really pissed off. So, they threw Jesus out of town – and told him to never come back. Mark also frequently quotes Jesus as commanding his followers to not tell anybody about all the people he cured and the other miracles he worked. Mark's gospel describes Jesus as more or less just a guy who wasn't quite sure if he was the Son of God or not.

While Ted was saying this, the camera focused on Mark – who had a look of "am I going to get to say anything?" on his face. Ted continued, and the camera switched to John's face.

Ted: At the other extreme is John, whose *Gospel According to John* is just about to be published. In this new version of the story of Jesus, John quotes him as proclaiming his own divinity every time you turn around. The Jesus that John describes is sort of pompous – making bold claims. In John's version, Jesus proclaims "I Am" …just about everything: the living water; the way, the truth, the light; the Son of God equal to the Father; the bread of life – just about everything you could imagine. In John's version, Jesus of Nazareth knew everything that was going to happen long before it happened, and literally everything in John's story of Jesus' life happened for a purpose ordained by God the Father.

Mark: Uh, Ted? Are we going to get to say anything?

Ted: Patience, guys. I haven't been in front of a camera for ten years now. I'm not going to miss this opportunity. And I'm on a roll.

Mark: I'll be patient.

Ted: So, before we ask these guys to comment, let me share with you some of my own thoughts on how these four guys could be telling such different stories about the same person. Suppose, for those of you that are watching this in the 21st century, that we wanted to pull together a documentation of the life of Franklin Delano Roosevelt. The reason I picked Roosevelt as the subject is because he had a profound impact on the world in our time, and because he died about seventy years ago. That's about the time span between when Jesus died, and the time that John wrote his story about him. So, think of it this way: suppose we were to hire four writers, and ask them to go dig up information on the life of FDR. If one of them was a historian, he might emphasize the facts about Roosevelt's accomplishments – just like Mark did about Jesus. Another writer might be a newspaper reporter, who approaches the story by interviewing those old timers that actually knew Roosevelt. So in this version, we see a more human interest side of the man – the one who needed to go to Hyde Park to escape from the pressures of the office. The third writer might be a dramatist, so he might write a play giving the life of FDR a dramatic sweep. And a fourth writer might be a novelist – and he might emphasize the conflicts that plagued Roosevelt as he dealt with the major decisions – and how did he manage to get Congress to go along with all the radical changes he made in how the country operated.

So, that's really the point. Four writers with four different backgrounds, acting independently of each other, writing stories about the same man. They are likely to all include a number of famous quotes from the man (for example, "we have nothing to fear but fear itself", and "December 7, a date that will live in infamy...") in their stories. But they would each emphasize different things about him – to the point that Roosevelt may come across as four different people in four different stories. I think that's what happened here with these four evangelists. That's why their stories are both the same and very different from each other.

At this point, the director started fidgeting in his seat, wondering if it was a good idea to bring Ted back from retirement to do this interview. He started remembering why he was glad that Ted retired ten years ago. Luckily, Mark came to the rescue:

> Mark: Who's this Roosevelt dude? Is he from Jerusalem?
>
> Ted: No, he came well after your time. It was just an analogy anyhow. So, Mark: your story was written first, and it is the shortest of the four. Why did you write it?
>
> Mark: Well, my community asked me to do it. They all were very familiar with what Jesus actually said. One of the people who were hanging around him all the time, a little guy called Schlomo, actually wrote down everything Jesus said, and published it. And in my community, people memorized everything Schlomo recorded. But, that's all they knew: *what* Jesus said – not *why* he said it, or the other circumstances in the life of this Man. So, they asked me to write down the circumstances – why he said all that stuff in the first place.
>
> Ted: Matthew, your story includes many of the same quotes that Mark attributes to Jesus, but you changed some of the quotes and emphasized different things. Whose version do we believe?
>
> Matthew: I had a copy of what Mark wrote, and I also had a copy of Schlomo's stuff. But, my community was middle class. And some of the quotes were just too radical for us. So, I just softened them a little,

that's all.

Ted: So, how do you know that you didn't change the meaning of what Jesus said?

Matthew: I just softened it a little. Jesus was a little too left-wing for my people.

The director sat up a little straighter, wondering if he should have bleeped that last comment. Would the left wingers among the listeners take offense? Or maybe the right-wingers would. He shrugged and decided to just let them carry on:

Ted: Luke, you turned the story into an opera, except without the music. What possessed you to put this kind of pomp and circumstances in your version of the story.

Luke: The folks in my community are all Greeks. They're used to a certain style when they read stories about important people.   So, I added a lot of heralds to announce that this Jesus was a really important guy before the story starts. All us Greeks do that in our writings. So, I imagined an angel named Gabriel, who appeared to Mary…

Ted: Wait a minute! You imagined Gabriel? You made him up?

John: I never heard of no Gabriel, man.

Luke: In my culture, the gods are always sending messengers to the key people in any drama. You should read Homer, Ted. He wrote epic poems about historical events with all kinds of made up people and made up gods and made up omens and made up messengers from the gods. Homer wasn't actually around during the Trojan War, but he was a hell of a poet. He knew how to tell a good story – even if he had to enhance it a little bit. But the Greek people are used to these literary devices.

John: Never heard of Gabriel, man.

Luke and Ted ignored John. So John returned to staring off into space. Luke continued:

Luke: You see, Ted, if you want everything to make perfect sense, you take all the drama out of it. It gets pretty dull. Look, I'm not the only one who took a few liberties. Just think about Matthew's version of the nativity. Do you really think that God led the Magi with a star? If you went outside and looked up in the sky right now and picked out any star - whose house would it be over? It's over everybody's house! Following a star is not very smart, but, that's probably the best he could come up with at the time to bring in some very important people to herald the birth of our Savior.

Matthew: Whoa! That's not fair. At least I didn't go crazy by putting singing angels all over the place.

Luke: So says ye who softened all the Lord's sayings. Look, Matthew was writing for the Jewish community, trying to convince them that Jesus was the Messiah by linking everything he did to what the prophets predicted about the Messiah. But, we're Greeks. We need little dramatic touches - like having a host of angels singing over the stable in Bethlehem… like having a lot of crowd scenes where the entire crowd speaks in one voice – like a Greek chorus in our dramatic plays. And do you really think Mary said that whole "My soul doth magnify the Lord" thing, and went on for the next twenty minutes without taking a deep breath? It's just how we Greeks write. Achilles kept talking for five pages at a time without taking a breath too, and then Agamemnon would talk for five pages, then Achilles would respond for five or six pages. That's just how we do it. So, Gabriel proclaimed Jesus as the Son of God, the host of angels proclaimed Jesus as the Son of God, John the Baptist did it too, even before he was born; Elizabeth did it, and Zechariah did it, Mary did it, Simeon did it, and all this happened before we even get to meet Jesus in my version of the story. That's just how the Greeks expect to read about important people. But, I don't know if any of these people or messengers even existed. I just made them all up to get the point across to my Greek community. This guy, Jesus, was really important. We always have relied on our authors and poets to use heralds, so we don't end up rooting for the wrong Dude.

Ted: OK Luke, thank you for your five or six page answer. You also explained why so many of your characters don't show up in anybody else's version of what happened. But that leads me to wonder how much other stuff you made up.

Luke: Well, I more or less cribbed the facts of my story from Mark. So, they're probably all true. I just put a Greek spin on things.

Ted: There seems to be a pattern of great religions cribbing stuff from each other. We don't know who started human sacrifice, but lots of religions took up that practice in the old days. And the Greeks and the Hebrews and the Egyptians all had their gods interfering in the everyday lives of the humans that worshiped them. And Luke and Matthew cribbed from Mark. What else did you guys crib?

John: You're not going to like this, Ted, but have you heard of the Holy Trinity?

Ted: Oh no! Did you crib that?

John: Well, the Egyptians had three gods-in-one over a thousand years ago. Isis and Osiris and their kid… I forgot his name… my mind goes blank every now and then… But anyhow, the Egyptians had three distinct gods, but they were also one god. I thought this was a really cool concept. Cool, man. But just because the Egyptians thought of it first doesn't make it less real – does it?

The director was getting fidgety again. Now he was starting to worry about the religious right – and he wondered how his ratings would suffer. What would the reviewers think of the direction this was taking? He wondered if he ought to break for a commercial and talk to Ted about the direction he was taking. While he was thinking this, Ted continued:

Ted: What else did you guys crib?

Matthew: The last judgment.

Ted: What?

Matthew: Yeah. Luke can verify this. If you read the tenth book of Plato's Republic, you'll see that Plato invented the concept of an immortal soul over a thousand years ago. He also described a judgment after people died, and they went to heaven if they had lived a good life, and to hell if they were bad. We Christians didn't invent that. Neither did the Jews.

Ted: Hmmm. All that cribbing is troubling. OK, let's turn to John now. John, you heard my opening comments about how you are unique in the way you have Jesus proclaiming *himself* as a Deity, unlike Luke, who had a bunch of other people do it for him. Any particular reason for this?

John: Nope.

Ted: So it just seemed like a good idea at the time?

John: You need to walk a mile in my shoes, Bub. You wouldn't believe what is going on in my community.

Ted: Why don't you tell us about that.

John: Well, first of all, we are mostly people who used to be Jews. But we paid all sorts of prices for our beliefs. The Romans leveled Jerusalem, and our temple, and we barely escaped with our lives. Then our own Jewish people disowned us because we believed that Jesus was the Messiah. So, they tossed us out too. We're all sort of bummed out about that, man. And many in my community are starting to question whether following this Jesus is such a good idea. They're saying things like: "He was supposed to save us. But so far, being saved hasn't been all that cool. In fact, it pretty much sucks, man. Nothing that we thought would happen actually did happen. The world didn't end. Nobody triumphed over the Romans. And following Jesus of Nazareth has been nothing but trouble. Now, they're martyring us just because we're following the guy."

Ted: So that's why you wrote the way you did?

John: I had this problem, man. My community needed bucking up. They were starting to think that all that stuff that Schlomo wrote down was all there was to the Guy – just sayings. All talk. I had to straighten them out. So, maybe I over did the "I Am" bits – but my people needed it.

Ted: Is that why your story is so anti-Semitic? You're pretty hard on the Jews, and you blame them for nearly everything.

John: The Jews were pretty hard on us – and they're blaming us for everything. This is just tit for tat.

Matthew: Yeah, but you go overboard, my man. Like you really got something against us Jews. Are you trying to get even?

John: Well, look at it this way, Matty. How can you people go for a couple of thousand years thinking you were chosen – singled out – by the one and only God – and not let that go to your head. Don't you think that makes you a little arrogant?

Matthew: Arrogant? First you blame us for killing Jesus, and now you say we're arrogant? You need a really good editor, man.

John: I'm just sayin'. That's all.

Now the director was glad he hadn't taken a break for a commercial. This was good stuff. People like to see celebrities tearing into each other. The ratings would probably go up now. Unfortunately, Ted was an old time newsman, and he cut it off:

> Ted: OK, OK guys – let's move on to another question. How about John's story of bringing Lazarus back to life. How come none of the other three wrote about that?
>
> John: You'll have to ask them, man.
>
> Ted: OK, you three, why didn't you tell the story of Jesus raising Lazarus. This happened when Jesus was on his way to Jerusalem – and it seems like such a spectacular miracle that the rest of you would have reported it to. So, why didn't you?
>
> Mark: Dunno.
>
> Matthew: Dunno.
>
> Luke: Dunno. Didn't know He did that. It would have been a cool story to put in there. It's got that Greek feel to it.
>
> Matthew: Hey Ted, can we ask you a question?
>
> Ted: Shoot.
>
> Matthew: You've obviously read all four of our accounts. What is your favorite part?

Ted: The Beatitudes.

Matthew: What's that?

Ted: The Beatitudes! They're right there in your Gospel. Also in Luke's. You know, "Blessed are those who hunger and thirst for justice…"

Matthew: Oh! You're talking about all that stuff Jesus said up on the mountain! But, Jesus didn't say "Blessed are those who hunger and thirst for justice." That is so lame, man. That's passive. Where did you get that? That must be a translation error. Hell, my stories probably got translated dozens of times before the version you think is the real Gospel.

Ted: So what did he actually say then?

Luke: Let me explain this one Matt. The word I used in Greek was makarioi, which must have gotten translated into "Blessed." That word comes across as so passive. But, if you go to Schlomo's text, which was written in Aramaic, you find that the original word was "ashray".   Ashray does not have a passive quality to it at all. Instead, according to my Aramaic/English dictionary here, it means "to set yourself on the right way for the right goal; to turn around, repent; to become straight or righteous."

Ted: Righteous?

Luke: Not like you mean righteous. The proper translation from Aramaic into English of what Jesus actually said would be something like this: "Get up, go ahead, do something, move, you who are hungry

and thirsty for justice, for you shall be satisfied. Get
up, go ahead, do something, move, you
peacemakers, for you shall be called the children of
God."

(Author's note: while I would like you all to believe that I
speak fluent Aramaic, and have deep insight into the
meaning of the original versions of the gospels, it isn't really
true. I stole that last bit from Elias Charcour, author of *We
Belong to the Land.* The cribbing continues.)

Ted: So Jesus was saying "get your hands dirty?"

Matthew: That's my take on it, right Luke?

Luke: Right Matt. Jesus was saying get off your
butts, don't be passive. Be active, energetic, alive,
and don't give up. You can make a difference. That's
what righteous means. It doesn't have anything to do
with knowing all the answers.

Ted: Well, I wonder what else has gotten screwed up
in the translation.

Matthew: That is a very good question, Ted. It is
worth asking that about nearly everything you read in
the Bible.

The director had been keeping an eye on the clock, and
noticed that the time was about up for this panel discussion.
He said something in a low voice, which was transmitted to
the bud sticking in Ted's ear.

Ted: Well, our time is just about up. And this is what
I heard from these fine gentlemen. They each had
separate motives for why they wrote their stories
about Jesus, and why they all slanted the stories a

different way. None of them intended to write a biography. They were simply reflecting the needs of their communities at the time. And so we get four different Saviors: an itinerant preacher, a guy trying to appeal to the middle class, a much heralded hero, and a Son of God. They all agree on some of the details, and have wildly different versions on other aspects of their subject's life. And the two thousand years of translations have not been kind to the original meanings.

One closing comment: Some of my listeners are very concerned over the apparent contradictions in the four Gospel accounts of Jesus' life. And, there are some doubters out there that favor conspiracy theories. These people want us to think that some Church person from the third century just made up these Gospel stories in order to justify the existence of the Church hierarchy, as a way to cement the growing power of the Church. After listening to our four Evangelists tonight, here's what I have come to see: It is the very inconsistencies in the four gospels that make them believable as accounts of the life of Jesus. If there were a conspiracy, don't you think they would have fixed the inconsistencies before they went public with the four accounts? The fact that the differences are right there for all to wonder about just reassures me that the accounts are genuine – not a conspiracy. So, I am going to go back and re-read these Gospels as a genuine representation of what the community of each writer actually believed about Jesus. Just like the Old Testament, the Gospels are a very human account of somebody's experience of God.

Goodnight Mark. Goodnight Matthew, Goodnight Luke. Goodnight John. Thank you for being with us tonight.

All: Goodnight Ted.

One of the screens started showing a commercial, and the Director slumped back in his chair. Half of the technicians lit up cigars and started chatting with each other.

Ted's last words lingered in my mind: *"Just like the Old Testament, the Gospels are a very human account of somebody's experience of God."* That doesn't mean that they were not inspired by God, I guess. Nor does it make them any less true. It does mean that in my search for "who was the real Jesus", I have to work harder to interpret what I read in the Gospels in the light of why those accounts were written in the first place. And the best I can hope for is to get the gist of who Jesus was, and an approximation of what he preached. One can still find meaning in approximations.

Questions for Reflection and Discussion:

-When I think about the words of Jesus as recorded in our modern translations of the Bible, how do I deal with the possibility that there may be biases or translational errors that have crept in over the centuries?

-If I set aside the notion that the Bible is the inspired word of God, can I still think of these accounts as a source of absolute truth?

XI. My Personal Pantheon

*What the Church says about God creating us "in His image and likeness" may be just the opposite of the truth. I suspect it is more accurate to say that we create Him in our own image, not the other way around. I have an entire pantheon of Gods I have created for myself throughout my life. Despite all my studies, **"who is God?"** remains a vexing question. The answer keeps changing. But the question I really want an answer to is this: **Does He know who I am, and does he care about me?** That is rightly the basis of all religion, including any religion based on an informed faith.*

We create God in our own image! At this point in time, we seem to be transitioning between a God created through the eyes of a serf during the days of the feudal system, and a God created by the offspring of helicopter parents.

The feudal system God was the one the nuns taught me about. For most of the history of the human race, the past 200 years being a rare exception, most of the human race lived under a feudal system. There were a very small handful of lords, lieges, emperors, or shoguns who all seemed to have gigantic inflated egos. The rest of human kind was taught to bow and scrape, to humble themselves, to constantly praise and glorify their liege lord, and to beseech him for favors, and also seek forgiveness from him for any transgressions. The ruling lord could make arbitrary life and death decisions on the fate of their subjects, with no consequences to themselves. It is understandable that we would create God in the image of these all powerful lords – a guy with an outsized ego who demanded worship and subservience and strict adherence to the rules, and who always seems to know what's going on with his subjects. That is the only system most people knew or experienced for themselves. So we made God like that too.

If we were to re-create God in the image of today's political system based on American democracy, we would elect a new god every couple of years based on what he pledged to give us. That doesn't make any more sense than basing our image of God on the feudal system.

The god we seem to be evolving to, at least based on a lot of sermons I have heard over the past five to ten years, is the god based on the helicopter parent model. Many in this current generation of Americans were raised with over-protective parents who don't want their kids to experience any form of pain or disillusionment whatsoever. This is the "god-just-wants-to-love-you" model. There are very few responsibilities for us in this model, very little accountability... just the expectation that we would somehow evolve into responsible citizens and be the helicopter parents for the next generation. And if we ever get into trouble or suffer any inconveniences, God will fix it for us. This model doesn't make much sense to me either.

When I think back over my life, I created a lot of gods along the way. The first god I created was only a slight variant of the one taught by the nuns. He ended up looking a lot like Santa Claus. (*He sees you when you're sleeping. He knows when you're awake. He knows when you've been bad or good – so be good for goodness sake – or you just get coal in your stocking.*)

When I was 8 years old, my nun-inspired-god was capable of loving me. He sacrificed himself for my sins. But he was also capable of condemning me to hell for all eternity if I died without first confessing my mortal sins. He was a confusing god at times, not above laying guilt trips on 8 year olds. The voice of that god was Fr. Saffin, my first pastor at Holy Family Church. I remember one of Fr. Saffin's Good Friday sermons that included asking us all to examine the palms of our hands – and then imagine someone driving eight inch nails through those hands. Wow, my sins created that kind of suffering?! But Jesus loved me enough to endure that suffering for me - personally. It was a hell of a sermon if I can remember the details sixty years later. And I must have been a pretty rotten 8-year-old if my sins were bad enough to cause all that misery to Jesus. Except I didn't think I was that bad. So somebody else must have been rotten.

There was a variant of nun-inspired-god that looked like Mom and Dad. I knew Mom and Dad loved me, even if they never actually said it to my face. I knew they had very high expectations for me. I knew they provided a secure atmosphere and all the opportunities I needed to live up to my potential. And if I screwed up, I had to sit on a chair in the corner and think about my transgression – and then apologize for whatever I did. I knew that Mom & Dad would protect me from harm – even if I wasn't the perfect child. And God was just exactly like them.

I really, really want to believe that God is a loving God, a helicopter god…like the one I hear about from the pulpit these days. God just wants to love me. He knows who I am. He holds me in the palm of his hand. He cares what I do. He is pleased with me. But I can't quite shake the image of God I developed in my early teens. I grew up the middle one of five kids. Nothing special. Kevin Leman, in his *Birth Order Book,* says that middle kids are like Rodney Dangerfield: we don't get no respect. As long as we keep living up to – or exceeding – expectations, there is no need for my parents to give me any special attention. They were preoccupied with much bigger worries than me. And, they were genuinely concerned that if they affirmed me, I would "get a big head." And that would be a bad thing for a teen-ager. That's what God was like, too. At least in my teen years.

That God of my early teen years hasn't ever completely gone away. I want to believe that God loves me, but this early-teen image of God evolved into a more troubling one: The Ant Farm God. This God loves his creation the way a kid loves his ant farm. There are millions of ants – and he loves them all. He loves watching them scurry around and

go about their daily business. But, they don't have
And when a couple of hundred of them die every da
big deal. A couple of hundred are born that same da
my big fear is that I am just ant number 376,217. Anc ..
participate in the activities of the ant farm. And some day, I
will die, and other ants will be born. And God loves all us
ants – all the same. He just doesn't know our names.

That image is very consistent with being a middle kid. It is
my own uncertainties about my own worth that I am
projecting onto God.

Now, as a recovering curmudgeon, I have a far less specific
image of God today. I can see his outline: a silhouette with a
question mark for a face – like on Facebook before you load
in a photo of yourself.

What is starting to sink in as I start running out of time in my
life is that my questions about all these Gods are very
similar. They really aren't questions about God at all – they
are questions about myself in relation to God. The questions
that trouble me the most boil down to these:

Does God know who I am?

Does God care what I do?

Does God really love me?

So, I need a new image of God. Here's my fantasy for how
these troublesome questions might get answered. Bear with
me while I add this new God to my pantheon: I'll call him the
Stay-Puft God.

This name is in reference to one of my favorite movie scenes
at the end of *Ghostbusters* – when the Stay-Puft
Marshmallow Man appears. In the movie, the Marshmallow

Man was about twenty stories tall, and he could peer over the tops of many of the buildings as he walked down the streets of Manhattan with a goofy expression on his face and wearing his sailor suit. In my fantasy version, Almighty God is as big and impressive as the Sta-Puft Man. He's just awe-inspiringly huge - an impressive 20 stories tall! You can't ignore him or pretend that he's not there. But he doesn't look like the Stay-Puft man at all. He actually looks like Michelangelo's painting of him on the Sistine Chapel, or maybe Gandolf, or maybe Professor Dumbledore. He looks like God ought to look.

So, my 20 story God is walking down the street and I'm watching him from the top of a 19 story building – just about eye-height. He stops and looks at me.

> God: I know you. Your name is Denie.

> Me:

> God: You have some question for me, right?

> Me:

> God: You want to know if I know who you are, do I care what you do, and do I really love you, right?

> Me: (slight nod.)

> God: The answers are yes - I know you. Yes - I care how you live your life. I want you to be both moral, and satisfied. And yes - I love you for who you are. You're much more than just ant number 376,217 to me. You're *my* Denie. I care about you, and I love you.

At this point, Almighty God smiles at me, taps me on the cheek, and continues walking down the street.

That would do it for me. That would answer all my questions. But what would be the consequences if such a thing were to happen?

My best answer is that I would no longer have free will. He would have taken that away from me in the process. I would have certainty instead. I would no longer have to wonder about anything. And perhaps, the reason why God doesn't do this, is that he *wants* me to have free will, and to choose Him just like (I hope) he chooses me – even though I still have so many unanswered questions about him. If I knew with absolute certainty that Almighty God holds me in the palm of his hand, there would be nothing more to choose. All the drama would be taken out of my life. It would be boring – like the guy on the desert island a few chapters ago. What would I have left to obsess over?

So, while I would love to have God give me direct answers, I am also kind of glad that he doesn't. I will continue conjuring up my God-du-jour pantheon – and then I'll die. And maybe then I will find out the truth. Or maybe not.

Uncertainty is the dilemma of seeking an informed faith.

Questions for Reflection and Discussion:

-How has my image of God changed over my lifetime?

-Who are the people in my life that most influenced my personal image of God?

XII: The Birds Coincidence

*Uncertainty is the dilemma of an informed faith. That leaves me perpetually wondering if God listens to me. And **does He respond?***

In the movie "Bruce Almighty," God asks Bruce to take his place while He went on vacation. Before long, Bruce's head was buzzing with a cacophony of prayers from a gazillion people. Bruce just goes to his computer and hits "Yes to All" – and all kinds of chaos ensues. The implication is that God shouldn't respond positively to every one of our requests.

But, this scene plays to one of my worst fears: my prayers don't really get through to God. My questions on this topic are very personal. It really doesn't matter if God answers other people's prayers. I want to know if He really hears me?

I should have picked "Thomas" for my confirmation name. Him I can relate to – the guy with all the doubts. My parents were probably too optimistic when they gave me a middle name of Joseph, the patron saint of trust. That one didn't seem to take.

One of the most troubling aspects of trying to have an informed faith is the question of whether my prayers are able to break through the cacophony in God's mind. I wish I knew for certain. He usually doesn't make things very clear. Most of the time, I can relate to the Pharaoh standing in front of that big stone bird, praying most fervently – while the bird just stares at him. Nothing comes back. Does God hear me or not?

I have been looking for proof – all my life, in fact - that God actually knows who I am. In the absence of the Stay-Puft God of the previous chapter, answering my prayers would constitute such a proof. But, here is where I am most conflicted. The real believers tell me that I need to be very still to hear the answers to my prayers. But whenever I hear a small voice in my head, I wonder if what I'm hearing is my own imagination speaking, or my own desires conjuring up the "right answer." Besides, most of the time, that small voice – the one that won't shut up – is cynical. That is not one of the attributes that Sr. Joseph Teresa taught me when she was describing what God was like in the third grade.

The real believers also tell me that sometimes God answers prayers by sending messages through other people. But then I wonder if they might not have their own hidden agenda in what they say.

In either case, it doesn't provide any convincing proof that God knows me, listens to me, and answers me. Maybe He does, and maybe he doesn't.

On the one hand, I would like to believe that God has been guiding me throughout my life – and answering my prayers in His own time and in His own way. People with a lot stronger faith than mine tell me that's how it happens. And I've certainly asked him to guide me often enough. But I often wonder if my successes are simply the result of making informed and intelligent decisions. I saved my money for college. I studied hard. I worked hard. I was prudent in managing resources. And at this stage in my life, I am well off. Was this due to God guiding my life over the years, or was it my own native intelligence that created these results? Sometimes, it looks like God opened lots of doors and windows for me. Those were His answers to my prayers. Other times, when the stone bird just stares at me instead of giving me answers, I think it all might be just my own doing. And I was just lucky because I prepared well.

On the other hand, there are many aspects of my "successes" that I know were not my own doing. I didn't choose to be born in America. I didn't choose to be a middle child, born of hard working, faith-filled parents. I didn't choose to have an inventive mind. Those were either very fortunate coincidences, or God chose those things for me. I could have been born into the Tutsi tribe in Africa with parents who were warriors, but not very good providers. I could have been sickly, and not very smart. Those would have been far less fortunate coincidences. And it leaves a lingering question of what God's plan might be for the people he had born into those far less fortunate circumstances. Did

God put me where he put me because he has a plan for what he wants me to do with my life? That would imply that He really does know who I am. And it may also be true for any random Tutsi warrior. Or, it may not be true in either case.

Here's my problem in a nutshell. I am hung up on the possibility of coincidences. Every time it appears that maybe God has answered a prayer directly, the scientific part of my mind always brings up the possibility it might just be a coincidence – and I just really, really want to believe that it came from God. When Dee and I were asked to be part of one of the Renewal Movements in the Church back in the 70's, was that the Holy Spirit moving in our lives (like they told us it was), or was it a coincidence? When the opportunity presented itself to move to England, and later to move to Connecticut, was that God opening a new door in our lives, or was it due to the fact that I got to be very good at my work – and people noticed?

Tangent: The dilemma deepens when I consider that if an answer came from God, then I am relieved of the responsibility for the consequences. It's actually pretty handy to have a God around to blame things on when I don't want to take the responsibility myself. But, I'm a responsible guy. I'm not looking to make God into a scapegoat – somebody to blame for my failures. I would just like some guidance every now and then.

So, I remain hung up on this. What is coincidence, and what is an answer to a prayer? The one coincidence that troubles me the most had to do with our decision to move to England. We were invited to move to England by an ex-boss, who wanted me to start an R&D lab and run it for two or three years. Was that a coincidence, or was that God moving in my life?

This new job was offered just before our family was planning to take a six week camping vacation - traveling through the American west. I told my ex-boss that we would use that six weeks to talk it over and let him know after the vacation.

While it was an honor to be asked, my wife Dee and I were very aware of how disruptive such a move would be. It would involve selling or renting out our house, pulling our kids out of their schools, saying good-by to our friends, and trying to fit into a new culture where we didn't know anybody. Our plan was to weigh the pros and cons during the long drive across the country – and come to some rational conclusion. Except it didn't work out that way.

We both tried to pray for guidance and wisdom in making the right decision, but we ended up spending the first three weeks of our trip fighting with each other. I thought moving to England would be a terrific adventure. Dee was more concerned about how disruptive it would be. We were at loggerheads. I was trying hard to see the situation through Dee's eyes, but I couldn't completely set aside my own desire to try this new adventure. We couldn't get to the point of rationally weighing the pros and cons of such a major decision. We got into character assassination on each other, and name calling, and – well, we were anything but rational in the way we were talking to each other. After three weeks of this, we calmed down a little, and started trying to determine if this move was what was best for us, our relationship, our kids, etc. Somewhere along the way, we laid out the question overtly: is this God's plan for us, or is this just another coincidence?

Late one evening we were driving our VW pop-top van up a mountain in California, on our way to Yosemite National Park. There was a campground halfway up the mountain, about a half an hour away from where we were. We had reached the point of one of those prolonged, stony silences – where neither of us knew what to say, and neither one of us wanted to be the first to break the silence. Our kids could sense the tension between us, and they were unusually quiet in the back of the van. I used that opportunity to pray (again) for guidance and help in making the right decision.

In the previous month, I'd heard someone talking about a prayer called "putting out the fleece." This is in reference to the time the Israelites were wandering in the desert, and they used a fleece – or a lambskin with the wool still on it - to give God the opportunity to talk with them. They'd put a lambskin fleece out at night and say to God: "If you want us to do option A, make the fleece wet in the morning. If you want option B, make it dry." Then they went to bed, and checked the fleece the next morning, and assumed God had communicated with them based on whether the fleece was wet or dry.

It was well after dark, and we didn't have any fleece in our VW pop-top – so I improvised. I asked God to give me a different sign: "If we were supposed to move to England, show me a bird before we stop for the night." I was giving him a half an hour to provide the answer.

I didn't tell Dee about my prayer. I didn't want to break the stony silence.

Well, here's what happened. We reached the turn-off for the campground, and I had not seen a bird. Now that I think about it, it was probably a stupid way to "put out the fleece" because birds don't usually fly at night. As we neared the campground, I kept searching the lights in front of the van for the bird – knowing it would be there eventually. But, by the time I could see the gates of the campground, no bird had appeared. I was bitterly disappointed, but I tried my best to believe that God had answered me, and He didn't want us to go to England. So, I swallowed hard and broke the silence, and told Dee what I had done. I told her about my fleece prayer, and how I had been looking for a bird, and I could see that as God's will for us – and He didn't show me a bird. I told her that I interpreted that as God not wanting us to go to England. There were tears in my eyes as I told her this. And Dee cried too. And we at least were able to hold hands as we approached the gates to the campground.

But, when we arrived at the gates, a sign said that the campground was closed. Everything was pitch black – and it looked like the site had been abandoned years ago. The next campground was another half hour further up the mountain. So, I turned the VW around and headed back out to the main road up the mountain. About thirty seconds later, Dee and I both saw a white bird fly through the light from our headlights. We both said "Was that a bird?" And as soon as we said this, a second white bird flew in front of the van.

I get goose-bumps even today when I think about this sequence of events. Was God testing me to see if I would take the "no bird" as an answer and accept it as His will – before he told us what He really wanted for us? Most of the time, I think He was doing exactly that. We did move to England, and we both believe that it was part of God's plan for us.

But was this a coincidence? This is the only time in my life when I actually believed that God was talking to us directly. (I suspect he may have simply gotten fed up with our bickering for three weeks.) If someone else were telling this same story, I would be thinking: coincidence. But the fact that it happened to me, and I had my faith tested to see if I would accept what I thought was the "wrong answer" leads me to think that maybe it really was God's doing. And when I look back at all the ways He used us to make a difference while we were in England, I tend to believe that He really did send us those two birds that night on the mountain.

So, here's the score: five million prayers, and one clear, unambiguous answer. One of the reasons I go to Church is because it is the one place in my life where I can get past my internal cynicism enough to hear a different little voice, a quiet one – which may well be the way God answers my prayers these days. Or, it might be my own imagination.

I have no idea of how you go about changing a confirmation name. Does anybody keep records of these things? "Thomas" remains the name of choice for me. The doubts may never be resolved – two white birds or not. But I am really glad they showed up that one time.

Questions for Reflection and Discussion:

-What doubts do I have that God hears my prayers and answers me?

-How should I be praying differently?

XIII: On Priests and Nuns

I have probably given you the wrong impression about my attitude towards the Church hierarchy. All of the perspectives in the previous chapters were priests and nuns as seen through the eyes of a school kid. It took me a while to learn to see them through the eyes of an adult. And this is an important point about a person seeking an informed faith: **it is important to look at the world through the eyes of an adult***. And that's not always easy. Here's my adult perspective.*

Being a priest or nun must be one of the toughest jobs on the planet these days. I make no excuses for the bad apples – the less than half of one percent of priests who did truly evil things, and the poor bishops facing incredible shortages of priests who didn't know quite how to manage the situation properly. But, that just makes it tougher being one of the 99.5% who have remained true to their vocation. My pastor notices that every now and then, a mother will make sure her child is safely behind her skirts while she is talking with him – not sure if he might be one of "those priests." I wonder how that feels – being condemnation by association?

Hold on a sec. There's that voice in the back of my head again.

"Denie,

Denie,

Measuring the Marigolds,

Seems to me you'd stop and see how beautiful they are."

Stop and see how beautiful they are? My great insight this chapter is that I spent a lot of my adult life looking at priests and bishops and nuns and brothers simply as authority figures. In my youth, nuns and brothers had the power to punish, and to judge you, and give out your grades to your parents. Priests were a little further in the background. They had the power to proclaim stuff. And forgive sins if you were brave enough to tell them what they were. And all these people were holy. Just ask my Mom. No, wait, Mom's dead. But, believe me, they were holy people. They all had vocations. They all were "called," and said yes. And they all asked me to pray hard to see if I had a vocation too. (I did pray. And I didn't have a religious vocation. I was too interested in tits. Actually, it took me until I was into my 60s until I could use that word out loud – tits - without wondering if a nun would do something evil to my knuckles if she heard me.)

So while they all had a profound influence on how I saw and interpreted the world around me, the nuns, priests, and brothers in my life were all a little distant. But, they certainly had my respect. So, what follows are three vignettes, and an editorial of sorts, on how I came to "stop and see" religious people through adult eyes - as human beings with beautiful souls.

Julian

One of my most unforgettable experiences was in helping a priest in England write his talks for the Marriage Encounter Weekend. His name was Julian. He was a parish priest in a small village in rural England. There were only about 75 or so people in his parish who came to his two masses every Sunday morning. Julian was quite short – maybe 5 feet 5 inches tall. He was just starting to go bald, but still had a pretty good crop of black wiry hair around the edges. Julian had what is often referred to as "that British Reserve." He had a dignity about him despite the fact that he was vertically challenged. And it seemed to me that Julian loved being a priest – for all the right reasons.

Back in the 70s and 80s, it was difficult for most men to discover that they actually had feelings – other than being pissed off at something. It was even harder for priests. So, one of the first talks on the Marriage Encounter Weekend, "Focus on Feelings," had both the husband and the priest share their own journey to discover their own feelings. For many of the participants on the Weekends, this was a real eye-opener. Hearing the men on the presenting team talk about their feelings made it easier for the participants to talk with their spouses about their feelings, and that set them up for many breakthroughs as the Weekend progressed.

Priests and nuns often came to experience the Marriage Encounter weekend for themselves, and many had amazing breakthroughs in their personal lives as a result. When that happened to a priest, he was often asked if he would like to join a team to present the talks on a future weekend. Julian was one of these.

My wife Dee and I had the privilege of "workshopping" dozens of priests around the world. "Workshopping" meant making certain that every talk on every weekend was the best possible talk that could be given. Workshopping was the quality control process. Our mission was to draw the best out of them – so they could put it on paper for their talks.

So, we met with Julian a number of times to try to get to know him. And just in the process of talking with him, it became clear to us that Julian was not a man who had ever been in touch with his feelings. His seminary training had convinced him that feelings were the work of the devil – and it was best to keep your mind on a high moral plain. So, we knew we had our work cut out for us.

Julian really tried hard. But, after several meetings and hours and hours of talking, he just couldn't see that he had any feelings, or any personal examples he could put in his talk. We were beginning to wonder if he would ever be capable of presenting on a future weekend.

Finally, out of frustration, we said "Julian, just tell us about your life. What is it like to be a parish priest in a small town in England." That's when we learned how much he loved being a priest. He thought of his parishioners as his family.

"What is that like?" we asked. He talked about how all week long he anticipates his family coming together on Sunday morning. He works hard to put together the best sermon he can give. He looks forward to the hour he can stand at the church door and shake each person's hand as they came into church. There was a twinkle in his eye as he talked about this. "So, that makes you happy then?" Yes it did. OK, that's a start. Happy is a feeling. Not a particularly relatable one for many people, but still, it was the first inkling that the man had feelings.

Then, on an instinct, we asked Julian what it was like on Sunday afternoon after his Masses were done and his people returned to their own homes and their own lives. He paused a minute. And then his voice broke a little as he said: "I go back to my rectory and I sit. And I feel utterly, utterly alone."

It turns out Julian had a beautiful soul, and lived in a lot of emotional pain that he didn't want anybody to see. And it was a gift to me because I so rarely see the lonely side, the truly human side of priests.

Oz

1976 was our Bi-Centennial year. Cardinal Krol of Philadelphia had persuaded the Vatican to let him host the Eucharistic Congress in Philadelphia that year. This was a really big deal. The Church only sponsors Eucharistic Congresses once every 25 years. It may have been one of the crowning achievements of Cardinal Krol's many years of service as an ordained minister. Hundreds of thousands of people were likely to come to his Diocese from all over the world. It was a huge responsibility to do it right – and the Cardinal was completely pre-occupied with the details.

The Marriage Encounter Movement wanted to schedule its annual convention in Philadelphia that year - just before the Eucharistic Congress – so that the twenty thousand couples who usually went to the convention could stay for the Eucharistic Congress. The Marriage Encounter Conventions were about learning more about how to love, and how to communicate that love. There were usually several hundred priests who attended these conventions along with the couples, and the couples were not shy about telling "their" priests how much they loved and appreciated them.

Three friends of ours – a couple and a priest – went to see the Cardinal to ask his blessing and endorsement of the plans for the convention. These three were from Philadelphia, but they knew Cardinal Krol only by reputation. He was thought of as a crusty old bureaucrat who had forgotten how to smile. A bit of a tyrant actually.

Our friends described the scene as they waited in the Cardinal's outer office the day of their appointment. The receptionist looked a little sour. But, they were impressed with everything else – especially the sheer magnificence of the décor in the Cardinal's offices. Everything was carved and polished dark wood, with indirect lighting, and plush carpeting. All three had very wet armpits. They weren't sure what they were going to say, or how they would begin. They had to keep reminding themselves that the Cardinal was actually a man.

When the door opened, they thought of themselves as Dorothy, the cowardly lion and the tin man, walking into a cavernous office with the great man seated way over there near the opposite wall. It seemed like it took them forever to walk across the room. All the while, the Cardinal was seated at his desk, staring at them intently, tapping the tips of his fingers on one hand against the tips of his fingers on the other hand.

The Cardinal said: "Why have you come to see me?"

And without ever knowing where it came from, the young wife blurted out "Your Eminence, we have come to tell you that we love you!"

The tapping of the finger tips suddenly stopped. There silence in the room seemed to go on and on. The three fidgeted a little, and strongly suspected that the Cardinal had never heard any of the people he had served all his life ever say this to him. They began to wonder if they had made a huge mistake, and maybe even doomed the plans for the convention.

Finally, with a lump in his throat, the Cardinal said: "What took you so long?"

What must it be like to be an important part of the Church hierarchy, and never know if anybody actually loves you?

The Tiger and the Pussycat

As I mentioned, nuns were authority figures in my life. Nuns were there to teach me arithmetic, catechism, phonics, and to condemn Elvis, and short-shorts, and any other near occasion of sin. All the training I ever needed to be a professional curmudgeon in my 60s I learned by the time I graduated from the eighth grade. To this day, I look at all the tattoos I see on young people - and what voice springs into my head??? – "You are the temple of the Holy Spirit." That used to be the reason for not writing stuff on the palm of my hand – but I am quite capable of extending it appropriately in my current world. Who knows what the nuns would have had to say about breast enlargement – much less all the free displays of the results - for me and the rest of the world to enjoy.

So, my lasting vision for the right way for the world to be came mostly from the nuns before I was 12 years old. I don't know how they got it to stick – but they did. And for the most part, I am profoundly grateful to them for my value system.

There were no nuns in my life beyond the eighth grade – up until I met two of them that came onto one of the Marriage Encounter Weekends where Dee and I were on the presenting team. Nuns and priests were invited to experience the M. E. Weekend along with the married couples because the weekend had much to teach about the essence of relationship. And in the post-Vatican world, people with religious vocations didn't know all that much about developing relationships with others. Most of them came from the pre-Vatican world, when such things were discouraged. So, many weekends had a pair of priests or a pair of nuns who were full participants along with the couples.

It was the first time Dee and I had ever had a pair of nuns participate on a weekend. But there they were. Early on in the Weekend, whenever I looked at them, the only word I could think of was "stern." And, I found myself hoping I wouldn't stutter when it came time to present our talk.

The participants on the ME Weekends write reflections to each other as an exercise after each talk. This is a useful tool for helping them be fully open and honest with each other in their communication. And the nuns also wrote reflections to each other. In one of the talks we were assigned to give on that weekend, we had to read out loud from our own reflections. And the subject of our reflections was our sexual relationship. It is one of the more vulnerable things a team couple is called to do as a member of the presenting team – and I found myself wondering how the nuns would react to hearing the two of us reveal something intimate about ourselves. When I glanced at them, they still looked stern.

So, I started to read out loud my reflection to Dee. It started "Dear Pussycat." When Dee read her reflection to me, she started with "Dear Tiger." And the content of our reflections dealt with how we struggled to communicate verbally with each other about some of the things that were way less than perfect about our sexual relationship. It wasn't a reflection about sex, it was a reflection about communication on a difficult issue, and a fear over how we each would react to the other's message. But still, not exactly material you would want even your favorite nun to know about.

We found out after the weekend, the two nuns told us they were inspired by hearing those reflections about our fears in communicating about our sex lives. It gave them the courage to start to share with each other some of the uncertainties they felt over whether their lives meant anything after Vatican II changed all the rules. It was a breakthrough for them to begin to address what had been a long festering identity crisis for them.

For the next twenty years, we received two Christmas cards addressed to "The Tiger and the Pussycat." It never occurred to me that nuns might dig romance.

Stern, my ass! It turns out that nuns have souls!

Editorial

"Seems to me, you'd stop and see how beautiful they are."

A few chapters ago, I had John the Evangelist comment that being the chosen people makes you arrogant. I think that happens to some priests too – who believe they were called to the priesthood directly by God. Some of them turned out to be righteous and arrogant – and hard to get to know.

But, I still believe that the call to priesthood, or religious life as a sister or brother, does come as a special calling from God. It is a small voice in the back of the mind that cannot be ignored. And, just like our experience of being married, the people called to the religious life go through phases of romance, disillusionment, and then evolve either into joy or misery.

Not so many are joyful these days. And those who are miserable have good reasons to be. If I imagine myself standing in their shoes, how would I react to all the insinuations of suspicion, the fact that so few people say yes to vocations to religious life any more, the reality that attendance at church is falling off a little more each year, and the whole brigade of Simon Cowell's in the parish who are determined to cut the bastards down to size? The clergy and religious people don't fare very well in the media either. The media is full of Madame DeFarges: tear them down. Tear them all down. Being a priest, nun, or brother these days is a real bummer. How would I feel in their shoes?

It had never occurred to me that Vatican II turned the lives of most nuns inside out – and gave them both the freedom and the burden of asking "who are we now?" Black and white turned to grey overnight. I didn't have any inkling that they were going through all that until getting to know those two nuns on our ME Weekend, and then reading a book by Sr. Joan Chittister.

If you're current on the media representations of this sad state of affairs, its easy to believe that our priests are failing us. Maybe its time to ask ourselves how we, the people of the church, are failing our priests. And all the other religious.

When I think about my current pastor, I wonder what his life would be like if he had ignored that little voice in his head calling him to be a priest. He certainly has the talent to be a manager in a large corporation. With the same amount of responsibility as he currently has as pastor, he would be a VP, pulling down a half a million salary each year, plus nice bonuses. He would have a trophy wife, two kids in Harvard, drive a Massarati, live in Greenwich CT, belong to a yacht club, etc. Instead, has chosen to give his entire life to us, his church – who imitate Simon Cowell for him every week, doze off during his sermons, gripe about whatever else isn't perfect, and treat him with suspicion.

I suspect Julian isn't the only priest who often feels "utterly alone." And Cardinal Krol isn't the only person in the hierarchy wishing someone would appreciate them for their humanity, as well as what they do for us. Maybe, as part of the way I live my faith, I should be making opportunities to corner our priests, nuns, brothers, bishops, cardinals, etc – and simply thank them for giving us their entire lives. Despite the fact that many seem remote, righteous, and sometimes arrogant, they are human. They have feelings and souls. I should be saying, and meaning, "I love you!" And if that feels awkward, then I need to spend some time thinking about why. What is it about me that makes it so hard to *"stop and see how beautiful they are."* That is precisely what a person seeking meaning through an informed faith should be doing. Practicing the faith in his relationships.

Questions for Reflection and Discussion:

-In what ways do I think about people with religious vocations as "them", and not "us?"

-What are some ways I am failing to practice my faith with the priests, nuns, or brothers I know? What should I be doing differently?

XIV. The Debate

*If you're still with me at this point, you would probably agree that I would not be a very good candidate for debating an atheist – or even an agnostic. I have a hard enough time debating with myself. In fact, I have been putting off writing these next chapters for a long time. I know I should have a good answer to the question "**why do I go to church?**" which is probably the first question an atheist would ask me. It will take me several chapters to get to this question, though, because I don't have a good answer yet. I know that sooner or later, I have to address this question for myself.*

Henry Neuman once wrote about a debate between himself and an atheist. I haven't read that book – but the idea struck me as a constructive way to address many of the unresolved things that have been rattling around inside me. Actually, its a cool idea! It won't *be me asking the awkward questions, it will be a fantasy atheist. I can save face, and pretend that I have answers. Despite my pantheon in an earlier chapter, or rather because of it, I would be a lot more comfortable if I had a good answer to the question **"What do I think God is really like?"** In this first part of the debate, I will use the fantasy atheist to help me to try to deal with that question.*

I don't think I've ever met an actual atheist. I know a lot of people who don't go to church, and who claim to be humanists. But most of the people in my life have always been church-goers, the kind of people who would find some of my *Drools* embarrassing. Most of them have very strong faith that reflects in the way they live their lives. So, to them, it probably looks like I have been leading a secret life by having some of the thoughts I have been recording here ... and if my faith-filled friends read this stuff, maybe they would think of me as a traitor – or worse yet, a hypocrite.

Who can I talk to about the perceptions of God, Jesus, and Catholicism that don't always settle well with me? I have had a few such conversations with my brother, Jim, who is asking himself many of the same questions. However, he lives six hours away, and the opportunities to spend time with him are unfortunately limited. The occasions for having long, in depth conversations with people who are searching for answers like I am, just don't seem to exist in my world. The Bible study classes I have attended at my parish seem to be filled with people of strong faith who are looking for reinforcement of what they already believe. Generally, I hate overly simplified pat answers almost as much as atheists do. But, since I don't know any real atheists, or seekers, or people who are into serious reflection on the questions that trouble me, I need to invent an atheist – and have a frank conversation with him. So I did.

My invented atheist looks rather normal, sort of like a college professor; with a neatly trimmed beard, wire rimmed glasses, and a pleasant disposition. I will make him as likable as I can. He's just a tad overweight, and dressed in a tweed coat with patches on the elbows – just to complete the stereotype. He actually smiles from time to time, but sometimes it comes across as a grimace. Every now and then, his eyes twinkle – but most of the time, he just looks serious and sad. I will call him Arthur, for no particular reason. (Actually, it's a pun. Get it? He's really just me.)

At any rate, let's see how this turns out. Here goes:

> ARTHUR: Let the debate begin! I just read the draft of your Drools manuscript up to this point. Why on earth did they send you, of all people, to debate me? You are already 90% atheist yourself.

> ME: Au contraire, mon ami. *They* did not send me. I sent me. And since I am making you up, I can put any words I want to put in your mouth - and who is going to know if it is authentic atheism or not? I, Good Sir, am holding all the cards.

> ARTHUR: The real atheists will know if whatever you're going to make me say is authentic atheism or not. So, you're not going to get away with that! (Hmmm – but on the other hand, what kind of atheist would be caught reading a book on a Quest for

Meaning through an Informed Faith? Maybe he can get away with it....) Anyhow, let me get the debate started. If you trashed the Bible so effectively in your earlier chapters, how can you believe in God? How can you believe in Jesus as the Son of God?

ME: Ok, I give up. The debate is over. You win!

ARTHUR: What?

ME: You win. I give up.

ARTHUR: So, what do we do now?

ME: Let's just have a conversation. A debate is a lousy forum for exchanging ideas. Neither party in a debate actually listens to the other party, except to think up ways to rebut what the other person is saying. I would rather we just talk – and try to listen to each other.

ARTHUR: OK by me. (I'll just quietly keep score for my own reasons. But I won't let him know I'm doing it.)

ME: Remember, I am writing your part as well as my own here. So, I can hear what you are saying parenthetically!

ARTHUR: Oh. Sorry.

We were meeting in the faculty lounge at the university - both seated in over-stuffed easy chairs. He was sipping a glass of dry white wine, and I had my gin martini. I would have had him puffing on a pipe if C. Edward Koop hadn't made that politically incorrect thirty years ago. Above all, my imaginary atheist is politically correct. But, I really didn't know him very well. So, I started probing a little:

> ME: Rather than rush into this conversation, why don't you just tell me a little about yourself.

> ARTHUR: What's to tell? I am an atheist. That's all that is relevant to this conversation.

> ME: Have you always been an atheist?

> ARTHUR: That's not relevant.

> ME: You should know before we start that in some ways, I am sort of an atheist myself. If you tell me about the god that you don't believe in, I will guarantee you that I don't believe in that god either.

> ARTHUR: I don't believe in any god. What kind of a god do you believe in?

> ME: That's why I invented you… to help me answer that question. But first, tell me what you do.

> ARTHUR: I am a tenured professor at the university.

> ME: Any family? Kids?

> ARTHUR: Also not relevant to the subject.

Maybe I should have invented a more forthcoming atheist. This one was not willing to divulge any personal information for some reason. Maybe in a later chapter, I will clarify why that is the case with him. But, luckily, he seemed eager and determined to get into this discussion.

> ARTHUR: You very artfully ducked my first question, so I will refresh your memory: "How can you believe in Jesus as the Son of God?"

ME: Before I answer that, let me ask you: do you think that Jesus was a real person – despite what the Gospels say about him?

ARTHUR: Well, I will grant you that a lot of people seemed to think he was a real person shortly after he lived. They probably didn't make him up. They also probably greatly exaggerated him. But, yes, there probably was such a person as Jesus, and he affected people. That does not make him the Son of God any more than it makes Thomas Jefferson the Son of God.

ME: Can't argue that point.

ARTHUR: And from what you wrote earlier, you and I seem to agree that the Gospel of Mark was probably the most authentic representation of the life of Jesus since it was written first. Agreed?

ME: Agreed.

ARTHUR: OK, so here are three things that should disturb you about Mark's gospel. Why does Jesus never call himself the "Son of God" in that Gospel? Why does he call himself the "Son of Man" repeatedly – almost like he is emphasizing that he is **not** the Son of God? And why, during the last supper, did he fail to say "Do this in memory of me" like he does in all the other Gospels? And why did the original version of the Gospel end with the empty tomb? The stuff about appearing to his disciples was added later, after the other Gospels were written.

At this point, I found myself wondering how did a self-respecting atheist come by all this depth of knowledge of the Gospel of Mark? So, I asked him if he had studied the Bible. He reassured me that it was important to him to know the subject thoroughly before he rejected it out of hand. He was asking good questions – ones that also disturbed me. I told him that I didn't have any answers. But I told him that I could add an even better one to his list.

> ME: When Jesus sent the apostles out two by two, was he trying to start a new church, or was he trying to reform Judaism? He spent a lot of time railing against the Jewish authorities who had lost their way at the time. So, is the Church even what Jesus intended?

> ARTHUR: You, sir, would make a fine atheist. Sign here, and we'll let you in.

Wait a minute. Are we discussing the existence of God, or the divinity of Jesus, or the legitimacy of the Church? I was getting a little confused, and I had accidentally introduced a new subject to the debate. And Arthur was leaning forward in his chair with a slightly smug expression on his face. I think he delighted in my confusion. So, I tried to get us back on track:

> ME: You're not going to sign me up because, unlike you, I have an unshakable faith in the existence of God.

> ARTHUR: And I have reached an unshakable conclusion that he does not exist. But, you have a scientific/technical background. And you seem to

have a big problem with coincidences – two white birds notwithstanding. Doesn't that lead you to at least question whether there is a God?

One problem with having a technical education and living among the technical community for forty-five years, like I did, is that I learned that there are very few things that can be accepted with absolute certainty. Over the centuries, most scientific discoveries turned out to be wrong – and replaced by later scientific discoveries which were also wrong. And, of course, there are all the sacred mysteries that the Church taught over the centuries – things they couldn't explain – and therefore attributed to God. Everything we cannot yet explain is not, therefore, the will of God. God didn't cause the plagues. Germs did. But the priests didn't know about the existence of germs – so they interpreted the plagues as the will of God.

> ARTHUR: Did it ever occur to you that I can hear what you're thinking just like you can read my parenthetical musings? Sacred mysteries don't prove the existence of God. They are just a label we slap on things we don't understand. You're doing fine, Church Boy. Sign here.

> ME: Wait. I'm just getting started. I agree with you on two things: First, everything deserves to be held up to rigorous examination, including intangible things like faith. And, secondly, blind faith is usually based on a form of ignorance – attributing things I don't understand to something I can't prove. But, I think there is a meaningful difference between informed faith and blind faith. I'm after an informed faith, whatever that is. I suspect if anyone were to scratch your surface, Sir, they may find a lost soul who would

really like to have an informed faith to hang onto.

ARTHUR: Maybe. But I have been through all that. There is simply no proof of anything you Christians profess to believe in. Including the existence of God. So, it's **all** blind faith, not informed faith.

ME: If there were irrefutable proof, we wouldn't need either type of faith. So, let's agree, we are not going to find absolute proof of anything. As scientists, let's shift the discussion to probabilities. What are the probabilities that there is a God?

I surprised him a little with that one. By the expression on Arthur's face, I could see that he was interested in exploring this approach. He was silent for a moment, lost in thought. Then he said:

ARTHUR: I have concluded that the randomness of the universe – and the facts of natural disasters - all indicate that there is probably not a God in charge of our existence.

ME: And I look at the *order* in the universe and conclude just the opposite. At a minimum, God is found in the laws of physics. In the 13 billion years since the big bang, the universe has evolved from incredible chaos into incredible order – with occasional disasters still happening every now and then. But we're moving in a direction toward more order, all guided by the laws of physics. But, where did those laws come from? Did they just happen, like the big bang? And what caused the big bang? Something appeared out of nothing. If the universe didn't exist before the big bang, where did it come from?

ARTHUR: OK, this is the 'God as First Cause' argument. Thomas Aquinas articulated that approach several hundred years ago. And I don't have an answer for it. But Aquinas' argument posits that there had to be a God that did it all – but that doesn't *prove* that God did it. Richard Dawkins did a pretty good job of refuting that argument.

ME: I don't agree. I wasn't very convinced by Dawkin's counter-arguments against Aquinas' proofs.

ARTHUR: Let's just agree on this: the science is just not advanced enough yet to explain how the universe was created or how it evolved. It's like what you were thinking a minute ago about germs causing the plagues, not God. We haven't discovered the equivalent cause of the big bang. But even if it was God that did it, I will point out that this argument makes God powerful, but not necessarily benevolent.

This man knew Thomas Aquinas' arguments? He was going to be a tough cookie to convince. But at least I had gotten him to acknowledge that there might be a first cause that is powerful. So, we had a starting point. But what he said about God not necessarily being benevolent was a point that had always troubled me. He was looking at me expectantly.

ME: Granted, there is no proof that God is benevolent other than anecdotal evidence. But, the fact that we are moving from chaos to order is some indication of benevolence.

ARTHUR: Harrumph!

ME: What?

ARTHUR: There is even less proof that God is benevolent than there is that he actually exists. At best, he is indifferent. Moving from chaos to order is likely to be another aspect of the laws of physics that we just don't understand yet.

ME: Could be.

Arthur went on to explain another problem he had believing the expanding universe theory. Science predicts we will eventually find millions of planets with intelligent life in our universe. We have already found a few hundred of them that have the potential to support life. Did God send his son to all of them? Or was our insignificant little planet orbiting an insignificant little star in an insignificant galaxy in an insignificant corner of the universe is actually the one place where God decided to intervene and send His son? Or does God have enough sons to send one to each planet? Or is he sending the same son to each planet to suffer and die all over again – once on each of the millions of planets with intelligent life?

That was eight or ten questions in a row. Arthur was starting to overwhelm me with his questions – especially since he was making a lot of sense in the way he posed them. I was starting to see that his atheism had not come to him in flash, but it was something he had spent a lot of time thinking about. I complimented him on his questions, and told him that I have no answers for any of them.

ARTHUR: Score another one for the atheist! As I have it, the score is now Athiest - five, Church Boy - zero! You're not doing much better than the Fundamentalists.

ME: We're not keeping score. We agreed that this is not a debate. Keep in mind, I am debating more with myself than I am with you. In fact, before you get too cocky, remember that I just made you up. And I can destroy you any time I want. I can be a benevolent god, or a vindictive one. So, you had better start letting me win every now and then.

ARTHUR: I thought I was already on my best behavior.

He looked a little contrite at this point. But, this was starting to intrigue me.

ME: OK let's look at your point about Jesus as one of potentially millions of Sons of God, each sent to a planet to suffer and die for our sins. That seems a bit improbable, I agree. On the other hand, who is to say that it couldn't happen.

ARTHUR: Let's stick with highly improbable. Besides, your Creed identifies Jesus as the *only* son of God.

I told him that we needed to call that question un-resolvable, and come back to what we have agreed on. First of all, we agreed that Jesus actually existed, and he had a profound effect on his followers. We also agreed that these facts do not necessarily make him the Son of God. We needed to go on from there.

ME: So, now the question for you, my dear Atheist, is this: Do you think that what Jesus had to say was worth listening to?

ARTHUR: Who knows what he actually said. The Gospels are not reliable, historical sources, as you, yourself, pointed out. Or was it Ted Koppel?

ME: Now we are getting into something I have been pursuing for the past ten or twelve years: what was Jesus' real message? Do you remember the "Jesus Seminar" back in the 70's?

Arthur recalled that the "Jesus Seminar" was a bunch of biblical scholars who concluded that what Jesus most likely actually said were the parables and the beatitudes. The beatitudes were a summary of Jesus actual message. And the things Jesus was *least* likely to have said was pretty much everything in John's Gospel. I personally found that a big relief when I first heard it. I've always had trouble with some of the things John wrote about Jesus.

One of the silliest passages from John's gospel was Jesus hitting his followers cold with "Unless you eat my body and drink my blood, you cannot have eternal life." This statement was attributed to him long before the last supper, when he introduced the concept of bread and wine becoming his body and blood. I always wondered what it would be like to be in the crowd listening to the great man speak – and then he starts talking about what sounds like cannibalism. Should I go up there right now and take a bite out of his leg? Turn into a vampire and suck out his blood? That will get me eternal life? Most of the crowd walked away when he said that. I probably would have too. Imagine if in the middle of his sermons on peace and justice, Martin Luther King had advocated cannibalism. The people would stop saying "Amen," and start saying "What?"

I related this to Arthur and told him that it was a relief to me to hear that most biblical scholars think it highly unlikely that Jesus actually said most of what is in John's gospel. This particular passage was most likely added to the gospel later - by some well meaning church person to justify the religious practices in his time.

> ARTHUR: My point exactly – the Gospels are not a reliable source.

> ME: I see them as a reliable record of what Jesus' *followers* think their communities needed to hear about him. But, I agree that somewhere along the line, somebody put a lot of words in his mouth, and attributed them to "God, himself," and then later declared that everything written in the Bible is the absolute word of God.

> ARTHUR: Agreed. It's pretty dumb to believe in a Jesus when we don't really know what he actually said.

Part of my problem is that I have been taught about this very tiny American Jesus – who is more or less the only one we still hear about from the believers around us. He is made in our own image and likeness. I don't believe in this very tiny American Jesus. I think there had to be much more to the guy, or he wouldn't have had such an impact on the world. As Richard Rohr says, spirituality is much more about unlearning than learning.

ARTHUR: So what does a person in search of an "informed faith", such as yourself, actually believe Jesus said?

ME: Well, here's what I think so far, after ten or twelve years of researching the question. Jesus' main message was just this: "Love God, and love one another." In His world, and in ours, that means sometimes rejecting the status quo, especially when it is mean-spirited and alienates people – the poor, the disaffected, the ill, the minorities, the women; in fact, anybody that did not perfectly align themselves with all the rules that the leaders of the chosen people decreed had to be followed. Jesus said that the laws of the church – in his case, the Jewish hierarchy – were **not** the absolute truth. They became a barrier to loving one another. Those laws did not come from God, they came from people whose motives were suspect, and who attributed their laws to God. Jesus taught compassion and forgiveness in a world where there wasn't much evidence of either – particularly from the hierarchy – who were mostly righteous people in the worst sense of the word. This more or less describes many of the current hierarchies in the religions around the world, and the attitudes of the righteous fundamentalists among us. The beatitudes and the parables are mostly radical rejections of the current thinking – in His world two thousand years ago, and even in today's world.

ARTHUR: Nice little sermonette there, Church Boy. But, I am starting to see your point. No, wait a minute…. What exactly is your point?

ME: Well, one thing that is most meaningful for me is that the Gospels never report Jesus as saying "Worship Me." What he said many times was "Follow Me!" Which, for me, is a matter of researching what he said, and then reflecting on it, and then acting on it – especially the greatest commandments of love God and love one another. I concur that his real message was wrapped up in the beatitudes, as the Jesus Seminar folks concluded. So, you and I need to ask ourselves this: Do we think that message is worth listening to?

ARTHUR: I don't understand the beatitudes. "Blessed are the meek," for example. This sounds to me like "Jesus, meek, and humble of heart..."

ME: Aha! An ejaculation! You must have been a Catholic at one point in your life.

ARTHUR: Possibly.

Hmmm. Another clue into the man I was debating. I thought that I needed to be patient, and eventually I would get to know his background a little. But, he started fidgeting in his chair, and I thought it best not to pursue the point at this time. So, I continued.

ME: Do you remember from my earlier chapter "The Sequel: Son of Evolving God" that I plagiarized a quote from Elias Charcour's on what the original beatitudes actually meant?

ARTHUR: Refresh my memory.

I explained: Elias Charcour sees the Beatitudes as calls to action. He says that the proper translation from Aramaic into English of what Jesus actually said would be something like this: "Get up, go ahead, do something, move, you who are hungry and thirsty for justice, for you shall be satisfied. Get up, go ahead, do something, move, you peacemakers, for you shall be called the children of God." The word "meek" is found in some translations, and the word "humble" is found in others. Jesus was probably saying that if you are going to make a difference in this world, be humble about it. Don't do it to toot your own horn. Somewhere along the line, somebody mis-translated all the beatitudes as "Blessed are you…" – and that just confounded Jesus' real meaning. Jesus meant the beatitudes as a call to action!

> ARTHUR: Hmmm. OK, so what?

> ME: So, I ask you again, my dear Atheist, do you think what Jesus taught was worth listening to?

> ARTHUR: I agree that his messages about acceptance, compassion, forgiveness, and his calls to actions are all good teachings.

> ME: So, if what he had to say was worth listening to and acting on, does it really matter if He was the Son of God or not?

> ARTHUR: Yes, it matters. Your entire church structure is built on an assumption that Jesus was the Son of God.

> ME: Ok, now you are asking a different question. Now you are asking if I believe in the "One, Holy, Catholic, and Apostolic Church" as we say in the creed.

ARTHUR: You seem to have your doubts.

ME: Well, I sometimes mumble that part of the creed when I say it.

ARTHUR: So, you **are** a hypocrite!

Now we were back talking about the church again, and not the basic question of what is the nature of God. So, I suggested that we save the questions about the church for a future debate, and tried to bring us back to the question at hand:

ME: Let me be clear. Do I believe in God? Yes! Do I believe in Jesus? Yes! Do I believe that Jesus was the Son of God? It's possible. But my faith does not hinge on that point. Do I believe that my church is the sole repository of absolute truth as the hierarchy often claims? I have my doubts.

ARTHUR: So I should stop calling you Church Boy?

ME: I still go to church.

ARTHUR: Why, for God's sake?

ME: For whose sake?

ARTHUR: Sorry, that just slipped out. Let me revert to type: Why do you go to a church that you don't believe in?

He seemed determined to get into issues about the church. It struck me that we needed to get into this, since his question "why do I go to church" is the one I have been avoiding for so long. So, I told him that this might be a good time for a break. I asked if he would like another glass of that wine?

>ARTHUR: Only if you'll have another martini.
>Actually, I haven't had a good martini in years. Was
>that one good?
>
>ME: Perfect!
>
>ARTHUR: OK, I'll try one of those.

As I walked over to the bar in the faculty lounge, I was glad to have a few moments to clear my head. I wondered: were we just going around in circles in this conversation, and not resolving anything? I guess I didn't expect to resolve anything – but at this point, I was getting a little frustrated. And I suspect Arthur was too.

Questions for Reflection and Discussion:

-What are some of the things I was taught about God and Jesus that don't always ring true to me? Why?

-What do I think are the most important things that Jesus taught? Why?

XV: The Debate - Round 2: Authority of the Church

As I carried the martinis back to our corner of the lounge, I started wondering if I should be feeling pleased with myself for holding my own during the first round. Actually, I didn't do too badly. My atheist friend was still a little stand-offish with me, but maybe the nice dry martini will loosen him up.

He wanted to take the conversation into a discussion of the church, and its flaws. I was not comfortable going there – it was one of those troubling questions I didn't want to face: **Do I really mean what I say in the Creed – that I believe in one, holy, catholic, and apostolic church?** *It was probably time to tiptoe into that question.*

And another looming question related to the quest for an informed faith has to do with the importance of doctrines. That was sure to come up. In my personal quest, I have always believed that it was more important to look at the intent behind the doctrine than it is to take the doctrine itself at face value. The intent usually has much to consider in terms of the values being proclaimed.

When I handed him the martini, I startled Arthur out of some deep thoughts he seemed to be having. That was good. Maybe I was causing him to re-think some things. Fat chance! He was probably just planning out his next attack. Even though I was just making him up, he seemed to be taking on a life of his own. Maybe I am not in as much control as I thought I was. So, I thought I would start out this round by trying to put him on the defensive, and seeing if I could pry a little more out of him:

ME: Cheers!

ARTHUR: Mmmm! You may turn me into a martini drinker again.

ME: So, tell me. How did you become an atheist?

ARTHUR: I told you before, that's irrelevant to this debate.

ME: Well, you guys are certainly getting aggressive lately.

ARTHUR: Who is "you guys."

ME: You atheists. A few years ago, 20,000 atheists descended on the National Mall in Washington to condemn religion.

ARTHUR: Oh yeah. That was that thing Dawkins did.

Arthur explained that Richard Dawkins is a British scientist who thinks he leads the "atheism movement." He has all the passion of an old fashioned tent revivalist. At that event in Washington, he encouraged his followers to assault the believers: He said: "Mock them, ridicule them in public!" Then he spewed out diatribes against the Catholic teaching on the Eucharist. It seems to me that what Dawkins has to say is downright mean spirited.

ME: I suspect Dawkins was upset with his publisher for not providing opportunities to promote his book — so he had to create his own event to get some press coverage. But still, the entire event seemed inappropriate for somebody who claims to use logic as his guide.

ARTHUR: Dawkins does not represent me as an atheist.

ME: But, it's a disturbing trend — this mean-spirited aggressiveness. Another thing: last year, the Wall Street Journal, the New York Times, and USA Today all carried full page paid advertisements with bold headlines asking "Isn't it time you walked away from your church? How much longer are you going to take this assault on your personal freedoms?" Why do you atheists have to put down the believers? There is clearly a snooty, superior attitude at work there.

ARTHUR: I agree completely. Atheism does not need a Jimmy Swaggart equivalent. We don't need to match you in righteousness and close mindedness. But, here is something for you to think about. It is possible that this rise in aggressive atheism may be the best thing that has ever happened to Christianity.

ME: How so?

Arthur explained that it took our very slow moving church hierarchy about 300 years to recognize that Martin Luther was one of the best things that ever happened to Christianity. Martin Luther brought focus to some important ways that the Church was going very wrong. He said that it wouldn't surprise him if we decide to canonize Luther in another hundred years or so. Then he added:

ARTHUR: But, here's my point; we atheists are asking some good questions. Unfortunately, some of us are doing it in the most obnoxious manner possible, with questions disguised as accusations and put-downs. But, if you can get past the method, get past your defensiveness, and actually think about what we are rejecting in your beliefs, it could do you a world of good. Our questions are exactly the ones you should be asking yourselves. You people may actually have to stop and reflect a little – instead of just spewing out pat answers. It's the pat answers that we atheists are most upset about – and you should be too.

ME: Point taken. I hope I'm not spewing out pat answers.

ARTHUR: No, you're a little weird… but no pat answers.

ME: So, what is it about people of faith that bugs you guys so much?

ARTHUR: There you go with the "you guys" again. All I can tell you is what bugs me.

ME: OK, shoot.

ARTHUR: Well, for one thing, I think religious people are simply delusional. Take my department secretary, for instance. She has her invisible Jesus who she thinks is always hovering over her, just waiting to straighten something out. She is always talking with him, just like Jimmy Stewart talked to Harvey the six-foot rabbit. She is a little bit of an extreme example – but I believe that most people with strong faiths are delusional in part. They think God is going to take care of everything for them. They see their religion as an alternative to taking responsibility for themselves.

If I had any say about it, I would send you all back to that old time religion where you had to save your soul, or you would burn in hell for all eternity. At least there was some sense of responsibility in that version.

ME: One of my problems with that old time religion is that it is based on the assumption of a vindictive God. I simply cannot understand a God who creates us, demands that we measure up to some very high standards, and if we don't, condemns us to burn for all eternity. I cannot believe in a god that is that sadistic and inflexible.

ARTHUR: OK, but the religion you replaced that one with is not much better. It goes too far in the opposite direction: you now say that God just wants to love us, and he forgives us even when we take no initiative or responsibility for ourselves.

ME: Yeah, I sort of covered this ground already in the chapter on my personal pantheon.

I couldn't help but agree with his point, though. His word "delusional" applies to many forms of religion – and to many people with strong faith. But I do believe that God expects us to save our souls.

ARTHUR: Save our souls from what? You ruled out burning for all eternity.

ME: Maybe our religion is meant to help us save our souls from despair and desolation. Maybe the real purpose of religion is to give us hope.

ARTHUR: Hope? Isn't that the same as delusion?

ME: You're pretty cynical, aren't you? Don't you have any hope? Don't you believe in the afterlife?

ARTHUR: Not at all. There is no proof of an afterlife.

Arthur went on to explain how the people who report the light at the end of the tunnel were probably seeing the doctor shining his flashlight in their eyes to determine if they're still in a coma, or dead. There are absolutely no credible records whatsoever that anybody has ever gone over to the so-called afterlife, then come back and reported that God was over there on the other side, and he welcomes us. All these stories are made up by the clergy to keep people coming to church to save their souls. It's not much different than the fantasy world of Harry Potter, with all the fairies and gnomes and house elves. Except that the church exploits its teaching authority. It sells indulgences to build cathedrals. It creates doctrines like purgatory and limbo just in order to have a stick to hold over people's heads. I objected to this. It was certainly true at one time, but there is no evidence that it is true in the Church that I know. Arthur countered with this: there is no doubt that the human race has a vivid imagination. There is just no proof that any of these fantasies about God or angels or heaven or the burning in hell or purgatory in the afterlife have any bearing in reality. They're just delusional stories. "Besides," he added, "you also covered this in your piece on the three missionaries visiting you on the tropical island."

I couldn't help but agree that there is no proof. So, I didn't know what to say about his points. He could be absolutely correct about some or most of them. But I challenged his assertion that the clergy makes up stories just to keep people coming to church. I believe that most of the clergy are incredibly sincere people.

I asked him what was his main issue with our church?

ARTHUR: Religion at its worst concentrates on excluding, condemning, threatening, judging, exploiting new lands and peoples, and controlling its own people by guilt and by shame. Your church has a history of trying to control what people think. You ban books, declare people who explore new ways of looking at the world as heretics, you excommunicate – throw out – anybody who does not toe the line – as defined by a group of senile old men sitting across the world in an ivory tower, paid for by atonement money and sales of indulgences. You mentioned those ads in the papers ... the ones that encourage your people to walk away from their church. Would you like to know why they're there? Your leaders have a pattern of forbidding everything. They seem a bit delusional too.

ME: I can't argue that my church has a colorful history, much of it embarrassing. But what do you mean that it forbids everything? What are you talking about?

ARTHUR: No pre-marital sex, no birth control, no masturbation, no abortions, no divorce, no canoodling between partners of the same sex... your priests and bishops seem to want to insert themselves into your bedrooms and control whatever happens there.

ME: So you reject the teaching authority of the Church out of hand?

ARTHUR: Don't you?

ME: I can live with an imperfect church as a source of sporadic insight and inspiration by simply redefining it as a human institution. If I needed anything to be perfect before I accepted it and embraced it, I wouldn't be part of anything at all. There will always be Lieutenant Fuzzes in the world – people who declare their own authority based solely on their title, or their association with other respected people, or by divine pronouncements. They're everywhere, not just in the churches! Accepting that there are some people in my church who are like that actually frees me to embrace what is good about our Church!

ARTHUR : I noticed that you artfully ducked my question again.

ME: Which one: the one about the Church forbidding artificial birth control and all those other things? This is an area where I actually have a positive opinion about what my Church teaches.

ARTHUR: How could you? Don't you see how restrictive and controlling that is?

I told him that when the Church first rejected the birth control pill, my reaction was to recall how they treated Galileo -- and most other scientific advances over the centuries. I thought that the hierarchy was just a bunch of old fuddy-duddies that seem to be automatically against everything that is new and different. I agreed with him that the hierarchy often felt threatened by new thoughts or inventions: concluding that they had to be bad for people. But, on this topic, I took me a while to even consider that they might be right – at least about the principles behind the teaching. And over time, I came to see the point they were making. Imagine that!

ARTHUR: Sounds like you're going to tell me how you came to this conclusion?

ME: Before I do that, let me ask you: where did you get the impression that my church forbids everything?

ARTHUR: Don't you read the newspapers?

ME: Yes, but, I suggest to you that the secular press is not the best place to get information about what my Church teaches. I expected that, as an academic, you would have at least read the original documents.

ARTHUR: What documents?

ME: *Humanae Vitae*, for example. That is the document written by Pope Paul that lays out the principles behind some of the church's teachings on the role of conception. Have you ever read it?

ARTHUR: I confess, I haven't. If I remember my Latin, Humanae Vitae means "on human life," right?

ME: Right. It's actually a very positive document.

ARTHUR: How can No! No! No! No! No! possibly be interpreted as positive? Your church is talking to you like you were all puppies about to piddle on the rug.

It has been over thirty years since I read the *Humanae Vitae* document, so I didn't remember the exact details. But I related to Arthur what I did remember: that the document lays out some pretty solid principles on the value of human life. It's actually a document Jesus could have written – if he knew how to write. It calls Christians to forsake self-indulgence, and set aside acting only in self-interest, and resist making personal decisions only based on convenience – and try to see the big picture... God's plan for the human race.

ARTHUR: If there is a God.

ME: Now you sound like an agnostic.

ARTHUR: For the sake of argument, let's pretend that there is a God. So, go ahead. Tell me more about this document.

ME: Well, let me ask you a question first. Do you believe that ecology is a good thing or a bad thing?

ARTHUR: What does that have to do with *Humanae Vitae?*

ME: Bear with me for a minute. I am going to try to describe my insight for you.

ARTHUR: OK. Yes, I believe that the human race should take a proactive role in protecting our environment. I believe that the Environmental Protection Agency, is one of the best things our government has ever created. I think that the success they have had in cleaning up polluted rivers and polluted atmosphere have not only been one of the best contributions of our government, but also long overdue.

ME: OK, so tell me – how did our world get so screwed up in the first place?

ARTHUR: I suppose it started with the industrial revolution – two hundred years ago.

ME: And what was it about the industrial revolution that led us to pollute our environment without thinking about it?

ARTHUR: Exactly that – we just didn't think about the consequences of our actions. I assume that you are leading me to conclude that the industrialists were acting in their own self-interest, and paid no attention to the prices others would pay for their actions. They didn't stop and think that they were violating the principle that our earth is a fragile eco-system that can easily get screwed up by thoughtless actions.

ME: Bingo! This was a historic clash of principles: creation of wealth, versus protect our ecology.

ARTHUR: OK. But, what does it have to do with *Humanae Vitae?*

ME: We aren't talking about *Humanae Vitae* yet, we're talking about the importance of principles.

ARTHUR: No argument from me. Life should be lived based on principles.

ME: Right! So we created the EPA based on an important and positive principle: take care of the earth. Don't mess up our eco-systems for the sake of convenience and self-indulgence.

ARTHUR: We agree on that. But I don't know why we are talking about this.

ME: OK, here's my point. I submit to you that there is an excellent analogy between the industrial revolution and the advent of the birth control pill.

ARTHUR: What?

ME: Hang on... I'll get to the point in a minute. You claimed to have read what I have been writing up to this point. Do you remember the piece about how we tend to create God in our own image – and the God we create probably has very little to do with the real God. We see God, not as he is, but as we are.

ARTHUR: Yes, I remember that one. One of your better pieces, I thought. But that doesn't mean that there is a God – just that we invent him to be what we want him to be.

ME: Well, here's one of my personal images of God. I am an inventor. So, I sometimes tend to look at God as more or less an inventor. A great one!

ARTHUR: OK, we'll add the inventor-God to our list of images that are wrong.

At this point, I told Arthur that I had a story to tell. One day, while I was walking on an abandoned railroad track on a balmy September day, I noticed that there was one of those fluffy seeds off a cottonwood tree that was drifting in the breeze and keeping pace with me. Somewhere behind me was a cottonwood tree that sent its seeds out on the wind. And somewhere ahead of me, that seed would eventually reach the ground, probably miles from the cottonwood tree, and might become a brand new cottonwood tree. And it occurred to me: what a clever and marvelous way for a creature to reproduce itself! Then I thought about blackberries. They have a similarly ingenious way of reproducing themselves. They wrap their seeds in a delicious fleshy fruit, which the birds eat and digest. The birds then fly away – possibly miles away – and excrete the seeds along with some fertilizer to help them grow. What incredible inventions! Our God has created such diversity in our world, and he has given every living creature a clever and often unique way to reproduce itself.

At this point, Arthur had a funny look on his face, which I interpreted as "why are you bothering me with all this crap?" I asked him to hang on for a few minutes, I would get to my point soon.

I continued my story: I then started thinking about the design of human beings. The invention of human sex is truly phenomenal. Women generate eggs, men generate sperm, and when the woman is most fertile each month, that is precisely the time when she is most sexually charged and open to having intercourse. Then, if she does not conceive, her body is designed to flush out the old egg and put a brand new one in place so she has the best chance of creating a healthy offspring by the time she is most fertile again in a month. As an inventor, I am really impressed with the elegance of this system. And in the male of the species, the drive to reproduce is even more spectacular. The most intense and pleasurable feeling in the whole gamut of human sensations occurs at the precise moment of conception. So, God designed us men with an incredible urge to reproduce, and rewards us with intense pleasure for doing so. He didn't have to design us like this, but he did. And we take this wonderful design for granted.

>ARTHUR: I already know this, and you're starting to sound like a stuffy professor now. I agree it is an elegant system. And human reproduction is fun, too. At least what I remember of it.

I continued my ramblings: that is what is most brilliant about the system. We humans have intercourse precisely because it is designed to be enjoyable. We often reach orgasm at precisely the moment that conception occurs. Fireworks right at the moment of a new creation. We are designed with emotions that cause us to fall in love and hunger to mate with each other; with brains that recognize that creating offspring is only part of the process, and protecting them until they are old enough to keep the reproduction cycle going for another generation is another part of the process. This is one of the most incredible inventions God has created. Our bodies and minds and emotions are designed to cooperate in the propagation of our species

> ARTHUR: OK, Professor. Can we set aside the argument over whether God invented this system or whether it just evolved that way? Otherwise, I am going to get defensive. Will you get to your fucking point!?

> ME: My point is that the birth control pill interferes with this process. It removes the reproductive aspect, and enables just the fun and games. It is the exact equivalent of the industrial revolution in that it enables us to act only for self-indulgent reasons. It violates a principle that we are meant to cooperate in the propagation of our species and replaces it with a principle that advocates self indulgence and just doing what feels good without paying a price for the privilege.

> ARTHUR: So, why did the pharmaceutical companies create the pill in the first place?

> ME: The underlying reason was to make money – same as the industrial revolution.

> ARTHUR: What is wrong with people who don't want to have kids having the ability to engage in intercourse without risking pregnancy?

> ME: Now we finally get to the point! That is exactly the important principle addressed by *Humanae Vitae*. We humans have a vital role to play in co-operating with God's plan for our world. If we interfere with that

role in order to be self indulgent, then we are screwing around with the natural order of things. Actually, I don't think the document used the words "screwing around," but you get my drift?

ARTHUR: I think so. You are saying that ecologists tend to howl whenever some company interferes with the natural order of things by releasing into the wild some hybrid critter that cannot reproduce itself. Likewise, your Pope said that we don't have the right to curb the ability of the human species to reproduce. My only comeback is that the pharmaceutical companies don't force anybody to take their pills.

This was true. But I mentioned that the document did not address the role of the pharmaceutical companies. I asked him to consider what happens in a world where people voluntarily stop reproducing. Japan and Italy are facing a crisis that will last many generations into the future. They essentially used the pill to stop reproducing, and now they have an aging population without much of a next generation to take care of them. This may be the law of unintended consequences, but if you scroll out 50 years in the future, it is a disaster in the making.

It was clear that Arthur had not thought much about this. He was starting to look intrigued by the direction this discourse was taking. So I continued with my opinion that people's motivation for voluntarily interfering with their own ability to reproduce is often self-indulgence. Having kids is a bother and an expense. It interferes with your ability to devote your life to your career, to climb the corporate latter, to create a comfortable lifestyle. It costs a hell of a lot of money to feed, house, educate, and nurture kids. And most of the time, it's not much fun. So, why bother if you have a pill that will enable you to not have kids – so you can afford to go out to elegant restaurants, buy impressive cars, live in great neighborhoods, and just enjoy all that this world has to offer? This is precisely the principle of self-indulgence. It comes back to bite you in the ass when you are 85 years old and worried about whether anybody will bother to come to your funeral – and what did your life amount to anyhow?

> ARTHUR: So, Pope Paul, in his role of EPA for the human condition condemned self indulgence as a principle in this document you've been talking about.

> ME: No, and that was my great discovery when I first read *Humanae Vitae*. The press reported that the Pope was saying No, No, No! What the Pope actually talked about in the document was the incredible role we have in co-operating with God's plan for his creation. He talked about the dignity and sanctity of a married couple in being the key part of God's grand design. He said that there is an important *principle* at stake here – that we were **made** to cooperate with God in the unfolding of his creation. The document proclaims the value in human life whether it is still in the womb, or an infant, or an addlepated geezer, or a mentally deformed person – all are part of God's creation.

> In other words, we don't have the right to screw up the natural order any more than we have the right to dump industrial poisons in the river just because it is convenient.

> ARTHUR: But what about those responsible couples who have had three or four kids in a row – bang, bang, bang – and want to take a break so they can

take care of the babies properly. Maybe they will have some more in the future, or maybe not. Shouldn't they have the right to decide?

ME: Yeah, that's one of the problems with talking about principles. You can lose sight of the real world. I struggled with exactly that question for many years. As a good Catholic, must I apply this principle in *all* situations, without thinking about it?

ARTHUR: Right question! How did you resolve it?

I told him how I stewed on this question for years – while my wife and I kept having kids. On one hand, one of my best friends while I was growing up had fourteen brothers and sisters, and they were some of the smartest and most well adjusted kids I knew. And I kept wondering: was I being self indulgent if I wanted to stop after four? On the other hand, wasn't my life stressful enough already? Did God want me to live in a perpetual state of tension and uncertainty over how I was going to manage to be not just a good provider, but also a good husband and good father when it was all I could do to keep myself from acting out my tensions on their little heads?

ARTHUR: Precisely my point. Isn't your church being completely insensitive by focusing on the principles, and ignoring the human condition?

I told him that he had just asked a great question. It brought us to another thing that is taught by my church. At the time we were wrestling with this issue, my wife and I sat in on a church seminar called "formation of conscience." The priest in this seminar clearly stated that decisions about whether to curb your reproductive ability for a time is not a decision that should be made quickly, or made based on feelings, or made based on the principle of self-indulgence. He told us we need to think about the matter carefully, examine our motivations, read *Humanae Vitae*, research what the church teachers have written on this issue, spend time discussing the issue with a variety of intelligent and moral people, pray for wisdom over the matter, try to listen to what God is saying in our hearts, and only then decide what is the right course of action. What the church objects to is making a fast decision or a default decision based on convenience or self-indulgence.

> ARTHUR: So, you are comfortable making up your own mind and possibly violating the teachings of your church?

> ME: The process of forming a conscience is never comfortable – at least not for me. I am always left wondering if I was just looking for a way to justify what I wanted to do anyhow. Once you start the process of forming a conscience, you seem to be faced with a series of agonizing dilemmas. But I do think that one of the best things my church calls me to do is reflect and pray – and try my best to call myself on my own tendency towards self-indulgence.

> ARTHUR: OK, good for you, Church Boy. So what about these bishops who make headlines by saying that certain politicians should not be given communion because they are not sufficiently anti-abortion in their public utterances. What about the bishops who are sanctioning the nuns – not for what they do, but for what they *don't* say? They're saying the nuns are wrong because they are not standing on soap boxes proclaiming the evils of birth control,

abortion, and gay marriage.

ME: All I can say about that is that my Church is not homogeneous. We have the equivalent of the Tea Party and the fundamentalists who are intolerant of nearly every deviation from how they personally interpret God's will. And they make a lot of headlines. And for some of us, they are an embarrassment because people like you assume that they are speaking for the entire church. And where in that do you find evidence of what we earlier agreed that Jesus, himself, taught: compassion for people who are struggling. It is true that our church is not a democracy; but you can no more conclude that every bishop who makes headlines by trying to beat the nuns into submission speaks for the whole church – any more than you could assume that Daniel Berrigan spoke for the entire church when he advocated civil disobedience and went to jail for protesting the Viet Nam War.

It can be quite frustrating. But, I believe that my church has not only the authority, but also the obligation to teach what it prayerfully perceives to be the truth. Is your University wrong, and should we reject and condemn it, when you have a right wing professor teaching something different than a left wing professor teaches on the same subject? They are both convinced they are right in their perspectives. With church teachings, I try to listen to what the various factions in our church have to say on the subject, but I also invest time trying to form my own conscience.

You buying this?

Arthur seemed to struggle to control a rage that was bubbling up inside him at this point. I was surprised at the intensity of his response. He went on a rant:

> ARTHUR: Not at all. You have way oversimplified the issue! Your whole point seems to be that a private conscience trumps any doctrine your Church may expound. Do you really think that your Pope and his band of uber-conservative cardinals would agree that private conscience trumps doctrine? Papal doctrines purport to be objective truth. They breach no dissent, ask no feedback, take no prisoners! Your bleeding-heart liberals accept formation of conscience as legitimate. But your real hierarchy wants to do the formation of conscience for you…. no exceptions! That whole free will and private conscience thing is just a damned nuisance for them.
>
> And not only that, but has your church considered that human reproduction is out of control?... as in population explosion… as in exceeding the carrying capacity for our planet… as in the ultimate cause for pollution and over-crowded cities and all… as in scarcity and competition for resources and the need for periodic war just for population control? Aren't those important moral issues too? It is true that China and Japan and Italy have a demographic problem because their birth rate is in decline. But have you been to Mumbai to witness for yourself what overpopulation actually looks like? Have you seen what it looks like when millions of kids are turned out into the streets to fend for themselves because their parents have too many kids to care for?

ME: Whoa! I agree that the issues you bring up are important. We clearly have a problem getting food and resources into areas of our world where such things are scarce. The question for me is whether there are alternative solutions to poverty besides encouraging poor people to stop breeding.

ARTHUR: What kind of alternatives are there?

I told him about a personal experience. I visited a Massai village in Tanzania a couple of years ago. The Massai people are cattle herders. They live about as simply as you can imagine. Their huts are made out of animal dung and sticks. They have no electricity, no running water, no refrigerators. Their kids people wear tee-shirts sent to them from the USA, and nothing else. No underwear or pants or shoes. The young men who graze the cattle all day have a cup of milk for breakfast, and then they cut one of the cows behind the ear and drain out some of the blood, and mix it with milk for their evening meal. They only slaughter and eat one of their cows twice a year, to celebrate their good fortune. They think of themselves as wealthy. The village I visited had a native population of about 150 people. Yet, they welcomed another tribe of about 250 people from Ethiopia, who were starving to death in the famine, to join them and share in everything they had. And they still thought of themselves as wealthy because they had enough to share with their guests. The guest tribe had been living with them for over three years.

ME: Your eugenic mind-set would say that if we had better population control, such poverty would no longer exist. Yet the Massai are truly joyful, welcoming, and loving people – who don't think of themselves as poor.

ARTHUR: I agree with your earlier point - that acting in a self-indulgent manner is not a good thing. But, I am not sure it is legitimate to focus on a Massai village and ignore the poverty in Mumbai and Delhi. Besides, aren't you allowing yourself to pick and choose among the things your church teaches? That doesn't make you a very good Catholic, does it?

ME: Ouch!

ARTHUR: You can't deny that your Church issues a hell of a lot of proclamations on a hell of a lot of subjects – and most of them are intended to control the spiritual life of the people who purport to be followers of Jesus. They are telling you how you should think! And your defense is that these proclamations need to be balanced with each individual examining their own conscience before deciding what to do. Isn't that like saying your Church is wrong?

ME: So, you think my wife should have simply started taking the birth control pills because there are too many people in Mumbai? For me, that would be just justifying my own tendency toward self indulgence for a good sounding reason. I think it is always healthy to look at the intent behind what is being proclaimed. The intent is usually right on target – and certainly worth considering. I am arguing for the value of serious reflection here. I concede that it is usually not a good thing when an important principle with an important intent gets translated into an inflexible law –

with no consideration for the real circumstances that people actually face.

ARTHUR: OK, I concede that too. You're probably one of those people who ignore red lights when you're driving at 2:00 am, and there's nobody else on the road. The intent of the traffic is to control traffic. When there isn't any traffic, do you still need to strictly adhere to the law?

I thought that was a bit over-simplified. But I asked Arthur to consider this: If Jesus came into our world today and proclaimed the exact same things as he said in the Bible – before his words were softened and edited and cleaned up for public consumption and lined up with whatever the Church happened to be teaching at the time of the editing, I would be willing to bet that He would be excommunicated from the Catholic Church and disowned by the Southern Baptists and half of the Episcopalians as way too radical. He would be considered an apostate. We would do to Him what the Jews did to him in his own time – throw him out and try to find a way to discredit him!

ARTHUR: Yeah – probably.

ME: So, for me, at least, trying to be a follower of Jesus means trying to fully comprehend what he taught, and what he meant – and looking at what my Church proclaims in that light. The bishops and popes usually have the best of intentions in what they teach – at least nowadays. Of course, our history is shameful in many areas, especially when the church became too political and obsessed with power and prestige. But that is not the church we have today. Yes, some of what the hierarchy proclaims comes across as rigid, self-righteous, and lacking in compassion and empathy. Jesus had the same problems with the hierarchy in his time. But he didn't walk away from his Jewishness. He remained a good practicing Jew despite the flaws in the leadership at the time.

ARTHUR: So that's why you stay? Because Jesus stayed?

ME: No, that's too simple. I don't know why I stay. I have been avoiding asking myself that question.

ARTHUR: Sorry – but it is THE question. It's the reason you're writing this piece. When are you going to face it?

ME: Next chapter, I guess.

At this point, Arthur had to excuse himself to go off and teach a class. I told him I would have another martini waiting for him when he returned. I was beginning to like this guy. He listened, but he wasn't easily swayed by arguments that didn't make sense to him. We did seem to be looking at each question from many different perspectives – even if we didn't resolve anything. I looked forward to continuing the debate.

Questions for Reflection and Discussion:

-What are some of the teachings of my church that I find hardest to accept?

-How do I reconcile the tensions between dogma and conscience?

XVI. Round 3: So, Why do I Keep Going?

As the professor was off teaching his class, I started thinking about how I have been saying a lot of things I am not sure I actually believe. Was I defending my church just because I was defensive, and I didn't want to let him score points? A part of me thinks that is precisely what was going on in Round 2. And I started wondering if I was being honest with myself.

While he was gone, I found myself thinking about how God never said the Church would be infallible or error free. The Church declared that about itself, and implied that the statement came from God. It occurred to me that as soon as I set aside notions of infallibility and freedom from errors in my church or her hierarchy, it was incredibly freeing.

187

The fact is, we will probably never get it right as a Church, and turn ourselves into the perfect religion. And that's OK. As soon as I reject the labels of infallible and "every word and action is inspired by God", then I can look at the church for what it is: a hodgepodge of truth seekers, controllers, formula creators, and formula-needers – most of whom are well intentioned, and a few of whom are confused, or in it for self gain, or self aggrandizement. We are a church of the saved as well as a church of the sinners. We just don't tolerate the sinners very well. And I personally find it even harder to tolerate the "saved."

So, I had put it off long enough. Round Three had to force me to address the question I had been dreading: **Why do I keep going to Church?**

I had another round of martinis waiting for him when he returned.

ME: So, how did the class go?

ARTHUR: I'm not sure my lecture came across very well. It was probably that martini that did it. Maybe this new martini might help me to recover a little! But, if I stop making any sense, we don't buy another round. OK?

ME: It may make the debate even more fun than it already is.

ARTHUR: You're having fun? Well, I guess I am too.

OK, Mister Pick-and-Choose Catholic, you *still* haven't told me why you continue to go to church you don't believe in. You just offered a half-assed defense of your church based purely on reason, but you didn't tell me why you put up with all the Hosannas and shit. You could have reached the conclusions you have been spouting without spending so much time on your knees. So, why do you keep going?

Me: Who said I don't believe in the church?

ARTHUR: You did. Earlier you said you mumble the "one, holy, catholic, apostolic" bit instead of proclaiming "I believe."

Me: Oh, that's just the tip of the iceberg. I don't believe the church has got it right when many of our rites focus on praising, adoring, and giving adulation to God. I don't believe in a God who expects that from us. That's a throwback to the middle ages when we likened God to kings and other royalty who had ego problems, and probably insecurity problems – who needed their subjects to bow and scrape and pay homage in order to feel like a king.

ARTHUR: Yeah, you said all that in an earlier chapter. But, don't you realize that you just rejected about half the prayers in your Mass.

That was true. I did. And half the songs, too. I admitted it to him, and added that I further reject the concept of the congregation as a flock of sheep. That may have been necessary in my parent's days when so few Catholics had educations, and they were not comfortable thinking for themselves. So, in that situation, following the rules to attain holiness was a comfort to the faithful. In my world, when so many Catholics are college educated, the strict rules that say everything is black and white, there is no room for gray – all looks exactly like what Jesus was railing against where the Pharisees made all the rules and ostracized anybody who didn't follow the rules precisely.

ARTHUR: So, now you just rejected about 90% of the canon laws in your church.

ME: I didn't reject them. I just think we need to look at the intent. But we addressed all that in Round 2. I believe that most of the Canon Laws were instituted for good reasons – just like *Humanae Vitae*. I am talking about the difference between blind faith and informed faith. With an informed faith, it is important to listen to what the hierarchy has to say, reflect on it, research it, pray about it, spend time forming a conscience, and then act based on the best interpretation I can make.

ARTHUR: Yeah, that's what you said in Round 2. So, you still belong to a church that rejects 85% of the nuns because of what they *didn't* say, who shuffles predator priests around and tries to hide them under the carpet, who pontificates on what it means to be holy – as if there is only one approved method, and who declares itself to be infallible.

ME: The church didn't reject its nuns. It was a few demented bishops who seem to have an authority complex. Well, OK, it was a *bunch* of bishops, cardinals, and, I suspect, even our ex-pope before he resigned. Well, actually, now that I think about it, they certainly did reject the nuns. So, I suppose I agree: your list of flaws in my church is certainly embarrassing.

ARTHUR: Yeah, these are the same guys that tell the nuns that they cannot be priests because Jesus had a penis. That makes as much sense as telling a woman she could never become CEO of General Electric because Thomas Edison had a penis.

ME: Can't argue with that logic.

ARTHUR: So, why on earth do you stay? You're all a bunch of hypocrites! Your central liturgy is built around a questionable assumption that Jesus was the Son of God, that he wanted his followers to "do this in memory of me" when it is questionable whether he ever said that, that he expects praise and bowing and scraping, and your priests seem to exist for the purpose of inserting themselves between you and your God – as if your approach to God isn't valid unless you do it through a middle man wearing fancy vestments.

ME: I don't think you want to hear my answer.

ARTHUR: With a scientific, questioning mind like yours, I most definitely would like to know why you abandon reason in such a silly pursuit. You're a little weird, you know.

ME: Because the church you are describing is the one defined by the press – who have to sell newspapers and attract viewers with scandals and other vile happenings. And many of those observations are completely valid. That's just not the whole story. It's not even close to the whole story. There is another aspect of my church that you don't know about. And the press doesn't bother to spend any time reporting it.

ARTHUR: I am only going on what I see. Are your priests still parading around in all those silly vestments, as if that gave them authority?

ME: You have a problem with vestments?

ARTHUR: They're silly looking.

ME: So, tell me. Why are you wearing that bowtie? Is that to keep your neck warm?

ARTHUR: Hmmm.

ME: It is a symbol. It says you are not working class. You are an academic. You are a thinker. So, you dress the part. That bowtie is only symbolic. So are the vestments. And those silly get-ups you all wear to graduation ceremonies look a lot like the vestments the priests wear at mass.

ARTHUR: Ok, one for the Church Boy. I lost track of the score anyhow. But I'm still ahead. So, stop ducking the key question! Why do you keep going?

ME: To tell you the truth, I'm not sure I really know the answer. But, here's some starter thoughts: I choose the Catholic Church – mostly as a stimulus. My church poses good questions and issues, and often challenges me.

ARTHUR: There are some academics of my acquaintance that play the same role for me. So, you could get most of that stimulation and challenge at a university. Besides, how can you overlook all the atrocities perpetrated in the name of religion?

ME: I can't overlook the atrocities. It is probably true that over the centuries, the number of people who have done evil in the name of religion far exceeded the number who were persecuted because of their religion. These are legitimate facts of history. If anything, this proves that the Church is not infallible, and we have done some awful things in God's name. But, those are just the things that made the history books. That is not the whole story.

ARTHUR: You're no fun when you keep agreeing with me.

ME: I'm not actually agreeing with you on this.

ARTHUR: So why don't you walk away, like the ads in the New York Times and those other papers encourage you to do?

ME: My country has done a lot of awful things too. I have not agreed with my country about 90% of the times we have gone to war. I don't agree with all the laws that are enacted. But, I don't walk away from my country when it's not perfect.

ARTHUR: OK, interesting point. But it's hard to not have a country. It's easy to not have a religion.

He had a point there, and he knew it. He watched me with a twinkle in his eye as I squirmed a little in my seat. I asked him to be patient with me, I was still processing this question in real time. Then I told him that, for me, the key question is what, and who, is the Church.

> ME: I submit to you, dear atheist, that the Church is not what you think it is. It is not the hierarchy, it is not the Vatican. It is me. Me, and millions of others – some of whom think they already have all the answers, and some of whom are searching. You are thinking only about the institution of the Church. I am thinking about my *experience* of the community of the Church. Big difference.

> ARTHUR: But you trashed the Bible, you trashed the liturgies, and you trashed most of the teachings of your church!

> ME: Au Contraire, mon ami, I did no such thing. I simply acknowledged what appear to be errors – something the hierarchy of my church doesn't do very well. Nor does the US government, by the way. Nor do most universities. My church is far from perfect. And if there were such a thing as a perfect church, I would not want to be part of it. Such a church would reek of righteousness, and I hate righteousness – which is little more than bigotry as far as I am concerned. And there certainly are a number of bigots in my church.

He was right about a number of points. I did trash the Bible. But, I told him that when I read it in the right frame of mind, the Bible gives me a lot to think about. It's just like the liturgies of my church: sometimes they touch me and influence the way I think about things. Most of the priests I know personally are actually inspiring role models who care sincerely about the people they serve. And many of the teachings of my church are incredibly challenging in a world where affluence and self-indulgence seem to be the holy grail. I suppose those are some of the reasons why I keep going to church.

> ARTHUR: OK, you said you reject the bowing and scraping in your liturgies, you reject a God that expects that from you, you question if Jesus actually said "do this in remembrance of me" – which is the central focus of your Mass. In fact, to me, it seems like your liturgies are little more than a bunch of people reciting prayers in unison, like a faceless Greek chorus, and not even thinking about what they are saying. So, what is there that's so good about your liturgies that keep you going back?

> ME: We've been over this already. Bowing and scraping is left over from the middle ages. Now, I agree that my church is a little slow in noticing that the middle ages are actually over, and we need a new paradigm. I suggest they look in the Bible and see what Jesus said about the nature of God. He called him "Abba", which translates to "Daddy." I suggest that would be a better way for us to think about God.

> ARTHUR: Yes, but only if you were lucky enough to have a good father. Many people were not so fortunate. Many didn't even know who their father was. What should their image of God be?

> ME: That brings us back to the principles expounded in *Humanae Vitae*. Men who impregnate women then skip town are an abomination. If we are living according to God's plan for us, we are called to be

good fathers to our children – to be a suitable image of God to them.

ARTHUR: Probably true, but I'm not buying this. What if you didn't know or didn't like your father. That makes a lousy image for God.

ME: What was your father like?

ARTHUR: He was a harsh disciplinarian. I never really knew him. He was always off on business trips, then cranky as hell whenever he bothered to come home again. Is that how you want me to think of God – as just like my father?

ME: Did he love you?

ARTHUR: I never saw much evidence of it. I suppose that he did provide for me. That would be one form of love. It just wasn't a very affirming form.

ME: So you would not have a very positive image of God if you patterned him after your own father.

ARTHUR: I don't think he gave a shit about me. There was nothing I could do to please him or have him take notice of me. Let's change the subject. I don't think I should have any more martinis. This is getting too personal for me to feel comfortable. God does not exist anyhow.

ME: Ok, so your relationship with your father wasn't exactly a good analogy for the way Jesus saw his "Abba." What about your own relationship with your kids.

ARTHUR: That's not something I want to talk about. So, make your point another way. What is it about your relationship with your kids that influences your version of the nature of God.

Hmmm. Another insight into my dear atheist. He didn't have any good male role models in his life? Could that have influenced his thoughts about God? I was tempted to pursue this further, but he was starting to get adamant – so I let it slide for now. I tried to answer his question by telling him about my own family.

I have four kids who are still alive. Three of them have started their own families, and two of them are in relationships that I do not believe are good for them. I ache for each of them to live their lives so that they feel a sense of fulfillment and satisfaction from making good choices and standing on their own two feet. Most of my kids seem to be doing that quite nicely for the most part. They have their ups and downs, days of satisfying accomplishment, and days of dejection. I celebrate with them when things are fulfilling for them, and I grieve with them when they experience discouragement, or pain, or even agony. But I know I have to let them go through it on their own. I suppose I could try to run interference for them and try to make everything nice, or even perfect for them. But I would far rather they experience their own senses of triumph when they face their adversities successfully. They might feel relief if I fixed all their problems for them, but I would rather they experience the sense of fulfillment, and sometimes joy, when they take initiatives and solve their own problems.

ARTHUR: And you think God is like you, as a Father?

ME: No, of course not. But I understand a little better how he might be a little stand-offish when things are not going well for me – instead of rushing in and fixing things, or responding to my cries for help. He wants me to stand on my own two feet, so he doesn't run interference for me every step of the way. God is not a helicopter parent... he wants me to live up to my potential. Maybe that's why it sometimes looks like he is choosing to not answer my prayers. Most of the time, the answers are already inside me.

ARTHUR: Interesting. You sound like you are blessed with a good bunch of kids. You must be proud of them.

ME: I have my days. Other days, especially when one of them never seems to get himself out of trouble, and keeps hitting me up to bail him out – I end up aching for him to get on top of things and have the pride of standing on his own two feet. These experiences just reinforce my conclusion that God chooses not to answer my prayers because he aches for me to get my own act together and become self sufficient.

ARTHUR: Hmmm. Maybe that's why he comes across like the Pharaoh's stone bird you referred to in one of your other pieces.

ME: Maybe.

ARTHUR: I can relate to the stone bird god. But, let's move on. We went on a tangent there, and you're still not facing the question of why do you go to church.

ME: OK, what was the next question you pelted me with a few minutes ago.

ARTHUR: You trash your liturgies.

ME: I trashed *bad* liturgies. Life is too short to waste it on bad liturgies. Going through the motions for the sake of participating in a rite can be a waste of time. There are a lot of things about my religion that trouble me – but good liturgies have never been one of them. Good liturgies give me energy and peace, and sometimes insight. And they reinforce my values. In our world, where else are you challenged to throttle back your ego and compulsiveness. Not on TV, not in the newspapers, not in college, not from the politicians, not from Wall Street.

ARTHUR: Now you are sounding like a preacher. I'd rather you stick with sounding like a Professor.

ME: That's exactly the point. Preachers, when they are good and sincere, have a message that you don't hear anywhere else.

ARTHUR: Like: put your money in the basket?

ME: Like, get over yourself! There's more to life than satisfying your own needs.

ARTHUR: Maybe I just never experienced a good liturgy. Give me an example.

An example. Hmmm. I thought about out how our Pope had washed the feet of prisoners, including women and Muslims. Then I described for him a phenomenal thing that happened to me one Holy Thursday. One of the portions of the Holy Thursday liturgy is the re-enactment of Jesus washing the feet of the Apostles before the Last Supper. I had seen this portion of the liturgy 50 or sixty times, and I understood the symbolism that leadership means service. But, a few years ago, our pastor invited me to be among the 5% of the congregation that washed the feet of all the other people at the liturgy. I had the privilege of washing the feet of my wife, then an Asian lady, a black teen aged boy, a Latina, a married couple (who offered to wash my feet too), and dozens of others who came to my foot washing station with tears in their eyes. I didn't expect that experience to get to me the way it did. It was a profoundly moving experience for me. I told Arthur that my church is the only place where I not just hear, but actually experience the message that real holiness comes from serving. Leadership is about serving, not self-aggrandizement! Everywhere else, I just hear just the opposite. I can't imagine Richard Dawkins washing anybody's feet.

> ARTHUR: Your church encourages you to wash each other's feet?

> ME: It is symbolic of the principle, like bowties. My church is the only place where I am challenged to make the values Jesus modeled for us into my own lived values. I go to Mass because it is a counter-culture to the things that pull at me every day: the American Dream, triumphing over others, and seeing myself as better than others.

> ARTHUR: Hmmm. I agree, washing each other's feet is a counter cultural message you don't hear anywhere else. So you had a strong emotional response to acting out this principle. But, to me, the

real question is how did this experience affect your life?

ME: That, Sir, is exactly the right question! If liturgies do what they are supposed to do, they affect how I live my life. After this experience of washing feet, I can remember several things in my life that I decided to change.

I told Arthur about how this particular liturgy affected my relationship with my daughter, who was going through a difficult time in her life at the time. Prior to that Holy Thursday, I had not been thinking about her difficulties. I had been focusing on the fact that I was a non-person to her. She had stopped greeting me when we were in the same room together. It had been months since she had initiated any conversations with me. She seemed completely self absorbed. And I had been reacting to all that by acting towards her in the same way: I stopped greeting her, and stopped initiating conversations with her – and I was cooperating in making the relationship cold and distant. I wanted to see if she noticed. And she didn't.

After that experience of washing the feet of the people in my parish, I started to realize that I was failing to apply this principle of "leadership means service" in my relationship with my daughter. I had been acting like a kid, as if I were self absorbed myself. And maybe I was. But, after that Holy Thursday, I decided to start acting like the adult in the relationship. I started greeting her, hugging her, and trying to engage her in conversations when she was open to it. These steps helped transform the relationship over time.

Arthur seemed to dismiss this as unimportant. That was just parenting. My realization that I was part of the problem in my relationship with my daughter was an important discovery for me; but I could see that I needed another example for Arthur. I suspect he didn't have any kids of his own, so this wasn't relatable to him. It also occurred to me that he had guided me to focus on finding a good answer to the core question of why do I go to church.

It occurred to me then that I had had a lifetime of Holy Thursdays, and reinforcement of the message that leadership means service. And those reinforced messages had, indeed affected the way I live my life. I gave Arthur another example – this one about my experiences as Vice President of Product Development for my company. For three or four years, I led a team of over five hundred engineers and scientists in developing forty or fifty products. I had a leadership team of twelve directors and thirty five managers on my staff.

The VP before me had left me with a morale problem. He had been inclined to deal with employee performance assessments by telling people they were lucky to have a job. But I brought the Holy Thursday mentality with me into the job, and I could think of several ways I tried to put it into practice with my leadership staff. I told them that we should treat each employee as if they were a volunteer, and we were lucky to have them with us. I told them that their role as directors and managers was to serve their employees. I asked them to think of the traditional pyramid as inverted, and we, the leaders, are on the bottom, not the top. Our function is to do everything we can possibly do to help our employees excel and live up to their potential. I even led the staff in conducting surprise employee appreciation days by all of us on the management team putting on aprons and pushing carts up and down the aisles to serve coffee and Krispy Kreme donuts to the engineers and scientists – and thank them for all they contribute. Morale improved.

I told Arthur that my faith doesn't mean anything if it is just in evidence at the liturgies. My faith is only valid if you can see evidence in how I live my life outside of church. Faith should be in evidence in the quality of my relationships with everyone around me. Faith should be evidenced in one's checkbook, and on one's income tax return forms.

> ARTHUR: OK, OK, OK – slow down a little Church Boy. I got your point. But, I submit to you that you could have found the same messages in thousands of books.

> ME: Maybe as a distinguished academic, you can read an important message in a book and make it part of your life. I'm not that good. I need to have the message reinforced. As the middle one of five kids, I am programmed to try to keep proving myself, topping myself... I am not inherently a people person. Relationships are a challenge for me. I don't instinctively know how to invest in relationships. I need the reminders, and I need them to be reinforced from time to time. That's what good liturgies do for me.

> ARTHUR: And you get those reminders in church? Maybe once a year washing feet is such a reminder; but I have a hard time, based on what I see in the so-called Christians around me, thinking that such a message actually influences most people – especially when they only hear it once a year, and only at so-

called "good liturgies."

ME: Oh, I hear the message lots of time throughout the year. Take Ash Wednesday for example.

ARTHUR: That strikes me as a really silly liturgy. The only thing that could make it sillier is if you so-called Christians started to wear sack-cloths along with those stupid smudges on your forehead. Isn't that just appeasement of your God – like you rejected earlier? "Oh don't throw me into hell, O God, just because I keep screwing up. See, I debase myself for your sake…"

ME: It is not about appeasement. When they put the ashes on our foreheads, they say "Remember that you are dust, and unto dust you will return." In other words, the clock is ticking, and soon each of us will die. Where else do you hear that reminder? The media tries to have us thinking of ourselves as immortal – with all the time in the world to engage in whatever self-indulgence they are selling that day. Ash Wednesday is one of the few times when I hear the opposite message: my time is limited. So, what am I going to do about that? It was in an Ash Wednesday sermon that I heard probably the most important question ever asked: what do you want them to put on your tombstone? What do you want them to say at your eulogy? That you were very valuable to your company? That you got revenge? That you made yourself very satisfied because you focused on your own ego? That "I did it my way?"

ARTHUR: Hmmmm. That is a great question... "what do I want them to say about me at my funeral?" What would your answer be to that question?

ME: Above all, I would want them to say that I was life-giving! That I gave my kids life not just by siring them, but also by loving them into life. That I gave life to my wife by finally learning to celebrate the phenomenally beautiful soul that she is and helping her to believe that about herself. That I gave life to others by learning to listen, withhold judgments, respond to their needs especially when there was nothing in it for me, that I learned how to be generous with my time, talent, and treasure. That I saw the time I have been given as a gift, and I tried my best to give that gift away. That's what Ash Wednesday calls me to think about. Above all else, it is a challenge to ask myself what my life means.

ARTHUR: Yeah, that's good. But I am not convinced that you need a church or good liturgies to live a good life. Most of the people I know don't go to church, but they are good people who care about those around them. Plus, you earlier questioned whether Jesus even intended to even start a church. You said he might have simply intended to reform Judaism.

For me, it doesn't matter whether Jesus wanted us to be good Jews, or become part of a new church. His messages were the most important thing. One of the things that leads me to believe that Jesus was authentic was the way his followers lived his messages. For example, over a hundred years after Jesus died, a Roman General named Tertullian looked at the community of people who were following Jesus teachings and remarked: "see how they love one another!"

It was enough to convert Tertullian to become a follower of Jesus himself.

> ARTHUR: We are not debating whether what Jesus said was worth listening to, we are talking about why you go to church now. So here's my real problem with that: I look at a diminishing congregation mumbling their prayers in unison, like a Greek chorus, as if getting all the words right and saying them out loud is what makes you holy – and I don't stop and think "see how they love one another."

> ME: Granted, many parishes have Masses like that. Some priests feel beat up, and are bitter and disillusioned and just going through the motions. And while I can't blame them, I would not want to be one of their flock. I have been in parishes that have nothing to inspire me. That's probably where my fear that I am just ant number 357,294 comes from.

> ARTHUR: So?

> ME: So that's not the whole picture. There is another side you don't see.

> ARTHUR: I need an example.

The best example I could think of is what happens after the Monday morning Mass in my parish. Usually three or four people who are facing operations for cancer or other life threatening maladies, and are scared to death, are invited up to the altar and given the "Sacrament of the Sick". The rest of the congregation comes up to the altar too and surrounds the people who don't know how they are going to face the realities they dealing with. As our pastor administers the Sacrament, the rest of us pray over those people. I can't say if God hears those prayers or not — or if the prayers influence the outcomes of the surgery those people are facing. It's what happens next that leaves a lasting impression on me. Every one of the thirty or so people on the altar starts asking about those that we had prayed over on *previous* Monday mornings. For the next twenty minutes, the people standing around the altar exchange news with each other about the people they continue to pray for. Some stories are heartwarming, and some are tragic. But, the atmosphere is one of compassion, caring, and a complete focus on those who are facing impossible odds. I leave those Monday morning experiences thinking: "see how they love one another." And Arthur would too. I told him about this experience.

ARTHUR: So?

ME: So, my church really does include at least some people who try to live what Jesus taught. Yes, there are some people are just going through the motions. But my church also includes the people who take food and underwear and toothbrushes to homeless people living under a bridge. It is the legions of nuns and priests who started hospitals and schools at a time when so many people couldn't afford health care or education. It's the Jesuit priest who nailed me to the wall because I wasn't listening to my wife and kids at a time when my career sucked up all my time. It is an imperfect, messy, sometimes hypocritical group of people — who are mostly trying to be on a spiritual journey. My church is not about ever getting there, it's about the journey. That's why I keep going to church.

ARTHUR: So, it's all personal with you?

ME: You betcha. Isn't your atheism personal to you?

ARTHUR: No comment. You're not giving me anything interesting to say during this round, Mr. Power-of-the-pen-person. You took all the good stuff for yourself to say. You're being a little selfish here aren't you?

ME: Sorry. Would you like to go on another rant or something?

ARTHUR: OK, here's my rant. I don't see where Christianity has made the slightest difference in the world. It is irrelevant, despite all the people who spend half their lives on their knees. Take Thanksgiving, for example. This is not a time where people actually thank their God for all the blessings. The Norman Rockwell version of Thanksgiving is gone forever. It is basically a feast of gluttony, and naps, and football, and arguing with relatives you only see once a year. Thanksgiving is simply the day before Black Friday.

And Christmas is another farce. It is supposed to be a celebration of Jesus' birth. But, basically, it is simply an excuse for shopping and avarice. You drive down the street and see how people have decorated their houses with lights and Santas and reindeer and big boxes wrapped like presents – and you never see a crèche – from people who profess to be Christians. What, exactly are they celebrating? The Japanese have got it right. They don't need Christmas as an excuse to exchange gifts. They do it because it is the end of the year, and they want to invest in their relationships with each other.

Christianity doesn't work. It never has, and it never will.

At this point, I told him how I spent Thanksgiving. The Sunday before, the people of my parish each brought a laundry basket full of food, and put it around the altar. We filled up half the church with baskets of food. The Monday before Thanksgiving, forty of us went to Mass, and then went out to the parking lot to start distributing the food. All morning, there was a constant stream of parishioners that pulled through the parking lot to drop off frozen turkeys and winter coats. Intermixed with them was a stream of people who were out of work, lost their houses, and didn't know how they were going to feed their kids, who also came through our parking lot to pick up a meal and a warm coat. We collected and gave out three truckloads of turkeys, probably eight or nine hundred baskets of food, and about sixty winter coats that morning. What was left over, we took to neighboring parishes in the poorer sections of town.

This did not make the evening news. Black Friday makes the news, including the big box stores that opened their doors on Thanksgiving Day.

The same thing happens at Christmas. People bring thousands of presents to be distributed. My wife and I buy dozens of pairs of underwear that get distributed to the people who live under the bridges, and who don't have the means to wash out their underwear – which they often wear for months on end. But, I agree: you don't see much evidence of Christianity when you drive down the street and see how people decorate their houses to celebrate what is supposed to be a Christian holy day.

> ARTHUR: So, being a bunch of do-gooders is what makes you Christian?

> ME: Let's see… the alternatives are to be do-badders, or do-nothings. Which of those would you prefer us to be?

> ARTHUR: OK, I got your point. You've actually done a pretty good job, albeit with a lot of fumbling around, of answering your own question. Here is what I heard. You go to church, despite all your reservations about it, because you need to keep hearing the key messages about your faith reinforced. You think that helps you to bring the principles of your faith into the way you live your life and into your relationships with the people around you. Going to church gives you time to reflect, and be inspired from time to time. And you go to church in order to surround yourself with others who are trying to live their faith, and be a counter culture to the messages you hear all around you in the media.

> ME: Thanks. That's actually a good summary.

> ARTHUR: Whose time to buy?

> ME: I've lost track.

> ARTHUR: OK, I'll buy this round.

Questions for Reflection and Discussion:

-What aspects of my church trouble me the most?

-What aspects of my church affect me the most?

Bonus Question (if you dare): What do I want them to say about me at my funeral?

XVII. A Somewhat Abridged Version of Church History

While Arthur was off getting the next round of martinis, I started thinking about what we had just discussed – the relevance of the Church. So, I'm going on a little tangent here. We will return to the debate in the next chapter – after I get something else off my chest.

Arthur rightly pointed out that we live in a time when a lot of the "civilized world" seems to be walking away from organized religion. And it is tempting to conclude, or at least ask if organized religion is now obsolete? John Lennon seemed to think so. His perspective is that religion does little more than divide people and set them one against another. There is certainly a lot of evidence for that. How can Catholics and Protestants spend hundreds of years killing each other in Ireland when they believe in the same Jesus – who notably instructed his followers to turn the other cheek? How can Shi'ites and Sunnis in many Arab countries take such joy in bombing innocent people that are not of their sect, but who praise the same Allah? Why aren't there more "Jimmy Carter" moments when he was able to bring together Christian, Jewish, and Islamic leaders simply because we all believe in the same God?

There also are a few other reasons – more cerebral ones – that are behind my own decision to keep going to church. They have to do with the history of the Church, which is often more embarrassing than it is enlightening. Even though the "truth in the facts" is almost always not the whole story, it is worth facing the facts for what they are. Then look for the deeper truths.

So here is my abridged version of the history of the Christian faith.

Even though I had a mostly Catholic education, my knowledge about the history of my church has been influenced more by the things I have read outside of my formal education. Almost all of them did not paint my Church in a favorable light – and rightly so. It is a completely different story than my Catholic education led me to think.

But, a visitor to the United States gets one impression of us as a people from watching all the crap we export in the form of entertainment, and quite another impression from visiting towns in the Midwest and getting to know our people and how they live. They discover that Chicago is not full of gangsters with tommy guns mowing down people on the sidewalks. And Dallas is not full of money grubbing oil barons. And most of the people in New York are actually nice people, not ill-mannered louts as they are often portrayed in sitcoms.

Similarly, the history of my Church is not the same as the history of the Borgias, the popes who decided to wipe out the infidels in the crusades, Spanish zealots who thought it was a good idea to torture people into conversions in order to save their souls.

But there are interesting insights that address the conclusions reached by atheists like Arthur and Richard Dawkins – that can only be understood by examining the history of my Church for what it is.

So, I would like to look at the three phases of Church history before reflecting on the Church as I experience it now.

Phase 1: "See how they love one another."

In the last chapter, I briefly mentioned Tertullian, a Roman Consul who lived over a hundred years after Jesus' death, and converted to Christianity after watching how the followers of Jesus behaved, and remarking "see how they love one another." I believe that how people lived in this phase was probably closest to what Jesus intended in his teachings. They really did turn the other cheek, and love their enemies, and sell all they owned and live in communities where they took care of each other. They followed the laws of the land, but they incorporated what

Jesus taught them in every phase of their lives. And it was there for all to see. It was the principle reason why the faith spread – a beautiful way to live amidst the ugliness that surrounded them imposed by tyrannical rule of the Roman Empire.

Of course there was dissention among their leaders - who were already declaring each other heretics for not interpreting Jesus' words correctly. Some of them thought that the real meanings of Jesus' teachings were hidden between the lines, and you only achieved salvation by breaking the code. So, they got thrown out. Others would give long sermons dissecting, parsing, and interpreting what Jesus actually meant – and they became the early doctors of the church. But it was not the leaders that caught Tertullian's attention – it was the people. They were the real church. They were what made Christianity *credible* as a religion. Always have and always will. The history books and the atheists just limit their focus to what the leaders do and say. Big mistake. They are not the church! We are.

Phase 2: Fear

I recently read Dante's *Divine Comedy*. It struck me that by the time the thirteenth century rolled around, "see how they love one another" had been replaced by the religion of fear. Dante, who was an ordinary layman/poet, both captured the essence of church teaching in his day (as distinguished from Jesus' teaching), and also created such a profound image of the suffering in hell and purgatory that it dominated how the Church thought about salvation for the next 700 years – right up to the Second Vatican Council in the 1960s. Dante's God allowed and enabled torture - for all eternity, for infractions against the rules. Dante's imagery was hard to ignore. He had sinners buried for all eternity upside down in human excrement. It was Dante that created the image of burning for all eternity. Dante's hell smelled of burning sulfur, and outhouses. Almost every imaginable form of hideous torture was to be found in all nine rings of the *Inferno*.

This was the dominant aspect of the Christian religion right up to Vatican II. In 1904, James Joyce devoted some forty pages in *Portrait of the Artist as a Young Man* to describing the first day of a retreat his character, Stephen Dedalus, attended at his Jesuit school when he was sixteen years old. That day of the retreat focused on a description of the horrors and tortures of hell – and it outdid Dante's version. It was so graphic and fearful a description that it led young Stephen to go immediately to confession. On his way, he lived in fear of God striking him dead – and thus he would die with mortal sins on his soul – and spend eternity in hideous tortures.

The religion of fear was certainly an effective way to promote the Sacraments, and instill loyalty in the faithful. It worked. Sometime during this phase, the Church evolved into an organization for sin management. The function of the clergy was to save people from the tortures of hell. The sacraments were available only through the clergy. The theology of Jesus coming to save us from this torture was promulgated from the pulpits. The abuses of power that led to selling indulgences all evolved from and were enabled by Dante's vision of the hell that indulgences were meant to help avoid.

Some Biblical scholars have speculated that it was somewhere about Dante's time that the words Jesus purportedly said to Peter were inserted into the Gospels:

"…who's sins you forgive are forgiven, and the sins you retain are retained." The biblical theologians in the Jesus Seminar think that this quote is one of the least likely things that Jesus would actually say. It is far too self-serving for the Church heirarchy. That quote neatly took the power away from God, and gave it to the clergy. It helped create a hierarchy that could rule by fear – even to the point of controlling heads of secular states by threats of excommunication. It was the clergy who could send you to hell, or save you from hell. And, of course, it kept the money coming in.

And it led to the "Kingification" of Jesus. He was no longer the lowly but radical prophet who challenged the morality of his day by encouraging his followers to respect and esteem and love one another at whatever price they paid for doing so. He was now a Prince, the King of Kings, who sat on a throne and expected worship from his subjects. One curious manifestation of this is found in a cathedral in Prague, where just above the crèche portraying Jesus' humble birth, you find an infant Jesus dressed in robes made of golden thread, encrusted with millions of jewels and an ermine collar, with a golden crown on his little head… just like the bishops and pope wore in those days. Apparently the people of Prague didn't think Jesus wasn't poor at all. He was super rich. He liked to dress up like Liberace when he was growing up.

This religion of fear persisted right up to the 1960s. In my own youth, it was common knowledge that you burned in hell for all eternity just for missing Mass on Sunday. That certainly kept the churches full. In high school in the late 1950s, I experienced much the same kind of retreats as James Joyce described – including the same graphic descriptions of hell, and the same fear of not getting to confession fast enough to have my soul cleansed of the mortal sin of having physical contact with a girl before I married her.

Yet, the people of the church I experienced while growing up in a Catholic ghetto were honestly trying to live a good life, treat each other with dignity and respect, be trustworthy with each other, help each other out when times were rough, and trust that God would provide what they needed. Looking back at that time in my life, I can't help but draw the contrast between how people actually incorporated their faith in the way they lived, versus the religion of fear that continued to stream from the pulpits. I strongly suspect that that same distinction (people trying to live a good life, versus the hierarchy attempting to control by fear) also applied in the time of Dante and James Joyce. It was the "big guys" who made it to the history books. It was the little guys, including most of the clergy, who tried to live their faith in a positive way despite the threats. They were, and always will be, the real church.

Phase 3: The Bubble.

In the previous chapter, Arthur comments on the streams of people who are leaving the church – and the Atheist Movement who takes ads out in the major newspapers encouraging people to walk away from their faith. Anybody who has remained faithful to most of the organized religions in their lifetime cannot help but confirm the validity of this "problem." This exodus started long before the clergy sexual abuse stories started making the headlines. So, why are people leaving? Are the atheists actually making inroads?

Here's an interesting bit of church history that helps explain what is going on in our time. If you remember the introduction to Section One of this book, I commented on how psychologists proclaim that our values and our perceptions of our own portion of the world are more or less set by the time we are ten or twelve years old. That's when "the right way for the world to be" is burned into our circuitry. The way the world was in our early teens affects the way we see and color and filter the happenings throughout the rest of our lives.   When the world evolves differently from how it was in that era, we assume something is wrong. Also, we tend to assume that our first experience of something is the way it is supposed to be. Its like the first winter after we moved to Rochester NY. It snowed over 200 inches that winter. So, that's how winters are supposed to be in Rochester. And every winter since then has been mild by comparison. One normal winter, followed by twenty-five abnormal ones.

The Church I grew up experiencing in my childhood and early teens was growing by leaps and bounds. My parish had eight Masses every Sunday, and there was never enough seating for everybody. Most of the side aisles and the vestibule were packed with people standing to "hear" Mass. So, the Bishop split our parish into three parishes in order to accommodate the growth – and he built two new churches in the area. He was also building new seminaries to accommodate all the young men who were studying for the priesthood. There were an average of 60 kids in the classrooms of my parochial school.   So, the Bishop built two new schools in the two new parishes. In fact, it is the legacy of my parent's generation that they managed the church through this period of unprecedented growth in the history of Western civilization.

But, looking at this era through the eyes of a twelve-year-old, I had no idea that this was an unprecedented growth spurt in the church... something that had never happened before. For me, it was just normal... the way things were supposed to be.

It wasn't until about ten years ago that I came to see how that period was not in any way normal. I didn't know that such an incredible growth spike had never happened before. So, why did it happen? In the forties and early fifties, millions of soldiers returned home from one of the ugliest wars in history. They experienced first hand many of the atrocities that Dante described as hell. They longed to have a normal life, practice their religion, have babies, and not go to hell for missing Mass on Sunday. If you could plot church attendance before and after World War II, you would see a hockey stick spike of impressive proportions. Church attendance nearly tripled in a decade or two.

It was like the stock market bubbles during the dot-com boom and the housing prices during the housing boom... when prices just went crazy for a couple of years. Then the bubble popped and prices for stocks and later housing just sank year after year. The same thing happened in the church. We are now simply on the other side of an incredible and irrational bubble in church attendance. It looks like people are leaving in droves – but what is actually happening is that we are approximately back to where we were before the wars. Many of the "bubble people" are dying off... my own parish averages about 200 funerals each year. We just have many more churches than we had before the spike – so they look emptier. We are in a consolidation phase. Where we split into three parishes during the upside of the spike, we are consolidating back into one parish on the downside.

Is that the whole story? Probably not. But it is a part of the story that I did not realize before.

Another part of the story is that the Second Vatican Council eliminated the religion of fear. You don't go to hell for missing Mass any more. Pope John Paul II said we're not even sure that Jesus taught that there was a hell. We don't believe in a God who enables torture for all eternity any more. We're trying to turn our heads around and believe in a God who actually loves us – instead of trying to dominate and threaten us. Vatican II was the Church's way of saying "we screwed up. We went in the wrong direction." True, Martin Luther told them that four hundred years ago – but at least they finally saw the light.

So, the people who went to church out of fear, and not because they wanted to learn how to live their faith more thoroughly, no longer had an incentive to go to church. I wonder if such people ever had a real faith to begin with. Many typical married couples with two kids these days are so exhausted by their two careers, frantic activities with the kids and other demands on their lives that church on Sunday becomes a burden if you don't go to hell for sleeping in the one day of the week when you can.

These three phases of Church history lead me back to the question: what is the Church supposed to be? I have mentioned that it is the people who constitute the church, but that statement is not intended to dismiss or diminish the role of the hierarchy. While the history books highlight the impact of bad management based on egotism in my Church, I am convinced that the hierarchy has always played a very important role – and they are even more important in this age of instant communications from everybody to everybody. Our world will always include kooks with impressive powers of persuasion – who can lead gullible but well meaning people to drink poisoned Kool-Aid in the name of religion. Or distort religious values for their own self-serving reasons. In a world that prioritizes self-fulfillment and self-indulgence over most other values, we need a Church hierarchy more than ever to remind us to live the values that Jesus taught us.

Despite all the headlines to the contrary, most of our recent popes and bishops – and most certainly our priests and nuns - have been doing a credible job of keeping Jesus' message before us. It takes a hell of a lot of courage to stand up and say something that the secular press will scoff at because it doesn't fit with the way the world currently thinks according to the charts on the front page of *USA Today*. The messages Jesus proclaimed in the beatitudes are still being preached, and are still as meaningful today as the day Jesus preached them. But such messages just don't make the news. And it is precisely because so many of the opposite messages do make the now ubiquitous news that the hierarchy of my Church still has a critical mission to perform. They are one of a very few voices of dissent – just like Jesus was in his lifetime – preaching the virtues of an alternative lifestyle. And living a faith does indeed require an alternative lifestyle.

I like where we are now. Most of the people who go to my parish are there because they want to be. They choose it of their own free will. And, as I mentioned in my comments to Arthur in the last chapter, there are even some signs that people are noticing the difference and saying "see how they love one another" once again. They want to bring as well as to receive. They are seekers. And that, in my view, is what religion is for... seeking.

Informed faith can only come from having an open mind. It is important to acknowledge your screw-ups, and find your way back to what is essential ... to what is invisible to the eye.

Questions for Reflection and Discussion:

-In what ways does my knowledge of the history of my church affect my faith and how I try to practice it? How balanced is my knowledge of church history?

-How are my expectations of liturgies influenced by what I bring to them versus what I get from them?

XVIII: The Debate - Round 4: The Unveiling

Before my tangent in the last chapter, my atheist had summarized what he heard me saying. I was starting to feel a little better about some of the questions that had been nagging at me. Now, I am left pondering whether the atheists in the world became atheists simply because they saw no evidence that Christianity was actually alive and well and working. They see lots of people going to church, but they don't see many people actually living their faith. When all they see are righteous people going through the motions of religious practices, I can see how they would question the value of that. I do too.

I noticed that the professor was a little unsteady as he brought back the next round of martinis. As he placed *a fresh martini in front of me, I found myself wondering once again **what actually makes an atheist tick?***

ME: We're getting to the point where if I say "Cheers", one of us is likely to spill something. I don't think I have ever had four martinis in a row.

ARTHUR: Maybe I'll just let my martini sit there a while and stare at your martini. Let's see....Where were we?

ME: Um, I think we were talking about atheism or something.

ARTHUR: There you go again. I still don't want to get into personal matters.

ME: OK, I remember now. Answer me this: you have given me hints that you once believed in God, and you once had a faith. What was it that caused you to change? What is your biggest hang-up with believing in God.

ARTHUR: Evil.

ME: What about evil?

ARTHUR: I cannot believe in a God who allows evil things to happen to people he is supposed to have created and cares about. That is mean and cruel. And while there is no evidence that God exists, there is plenty of evidence that evil things happen to good people.

ME: I get hung up on that too. I can only deal with it philosophically.

ARTHUR: How so?

ME: You've read Aldous Huxley's *Brave New World*?

ARTHUR: Years ago.

ME: Me too. The world Huxley created was weird, wasn't it? Its population had all the stress removed from their lives. They don't have kids – that's all done in a laboratory. They get up, go to their jobs, do mind numbing work, they come home and zone out on soma – a drug that lets them experience a night of pleasant bliss. They want nothing, feel nothing, love nothing, feel no love in their lives, and just keep doing the same thing year after year.

ARTHUR: Your point?

ME: For some reason, God gave us free will – the right to choose and determine our own course, and deal with the ugly sides of our world. Our world is full of pain and suffering – because God designed us with emotions.

ARTHUR: If God does exist, that was probably his biggesht mishtake. Did I just say mishtake?

ME: I don't know. Shounded fine to me.

ARTHUR: Go on, my good man.

ME: I shall, my dear Atheist. Anyhow, for whatever reason, God designed us with brains, and emotions, and free will – and so, our lives are full of contrasts: pain and joy, love and indifference, celebration and dejection. Take away the free will and emotions, and you have *Brave New World* – where nobody ever feels anything. If I were God, I'm not sure I would have taken the risk to allow people the freedom to do evil things, to hurt one another, pay prices for their own actions, and the thoughtlessness of others. If I were God, I might have been tempted to design people like the ant farms: you're born, you do your work, then you die.

ARTHUR: You're right, my man. You are a philosopher! But, if it were a choice of feeling pain versus feeling nothing, I'm not sure which I would choose.

ME: You would choose the ant farm?

ARTHUR: I might have already chosen it.

ME: Spoken like a man in a lot of pain.

ARTHUR: You're getting personal again. Let's just schtick with my point that I cannot accept a God who allows evil and cruel things to happen to his creatures.

ME: But that is just part of the human condition. At least it's not mind numbing. Can I ask you again: do you have a family?

ARTHUR: My students are my family.

ME: Do they love you?

ARTHUR: They tolerate me. It's hard to love somebody who affects your future and has the power to give low grades.

ME: That's kind of sad. It sounds like your life might be a journey of pain avoidance.

ARTHUR: That's personal.

ME: So, you have nobody in your life that loves you?

ARTHUR: Stop with the personal questions.

ME: I suspect that something happened in your life that turned you against God. And it turned you against letting yourself be loved at the same time.

ARTHUR: God doesn't exist.

ME: Let me tell you a personal story. I almost turned against God once. And it didn't really help me feel better. I was just so angry with him that he would allow evil things to happen to his creatures, as you put it.

My wife was eight months pregnant with our fifth child – a little boy. We had already named him Christopher, even before he was born.

ARTHUR: Christopher? Oh no!

ME: What's wrong?

ARTHUR: Nothing. Just tell your story.

ME: OK. It was a time in my life when I was travelling a lot. I missed being home with my wife and kids, and I was pretty stressed out. I had a trip scheduled to go to Germany, and so my wife and I asked her doctor if she could accompany me on that trip even though she was eight months pregnant. He said it would be OK, just don't push it – and let her get lots of rest. Well, the baby came while we were in Germany – except he was born dead. He was a perfectly healthy little boy, except he strangled on the cord during the birth process.

ARTHUR: I'm so sorry.

ME: That evening, after my wife fell asleep, I walked the streets of Hanover, Germany trying to make sense of it all, and trying to deal with my own emotions. I ended up yelling at God for being so cruel. How could he have done that to an innocent child? How could he do that to my wife! Was he punishing me for being so stupid and selfish as to want her to come to Germany with me when she was eight months pregnant? Why take it out on a baby who never did anything to deserve such treatment?

When I returned to the hospital, my wife was awake – and we spent the rest of the evening crying together – and not knowing what to say to each other. All we could do was hold each other and cry.

Christopher would be in a University right now had he lived. He might have even been one of your students.

So, tell me, where was God in all that?

ARTHUR: You are asking this question of an atheist?

ME: Sorry. No, I am probably still asking it to myself.

ARTHUR: How did you get over that experience?

ME: I didn't. I still have no answer for why God allows his people to feel such pain. My Brave New World philosophical crap doesn't help me to cope with this.

ARTHUR: So, you are still angry with God?

ME:

ARTHUR: Do you need a minute?

ME: I'm OK.

ARTHUR: Your story touched me. I am sorry for your loss. I do have an answer to your question though.

ME:

ARTHUR: Do you want to hear it?

ME: I don't understand God. I think it was Christopher's death that lead me to ask myself again and again whether God really cares about me, and what I do. That's probably why I started to think of myself as one of the ants on his ant farm. He doesn't care if one of his baby ants die. There will be lots of other baby ants. To this day, it is hard for me to believe that God takes a personal interest in me, and I don't know how to resolve that. (Pause) ...wait a minute. What did you say?

ARTHUR: Do you want to hear an answer to your question?

ME: What question?

ARTHUR: Where was God in all that?

ME: You have an answer for that question?

ARTHUR: Something for you to consider. Has it ever occurred to you how much worse that situation could have been?

ME: Worse, how?

ARTHUR: If your wife had *not* been with you in Germany, and the baby died while she was in this country and you were in Germany, can you imagine how that would have felt? At least you had each other to cry with.

ME: I never thought of it that way.

ARTHUR: Maybe God is in the relationship you have with your wife.

ME: I certainly felt better when I was crying with her than I did when I was on my own walking the streets and yelling at God.

ARTHUR: Don't tell anybody I said that.

ME: Your secret is safe with me. It sounds like you might still be searching for answers.

ARTHUR: I gave up searching for answers.

ME: Why?

ARTHUR: You're going to keep pestering me for personal details until I tell you, aren't you?

ME: I don't want to make you uncomfortable.

ARTHUR: I had a baby boy once. And his name was Christopher too.

ME: No kidding. You're married then?

ARTHUR: Was.

ME: Can you tell me about that?

ARTHUR: (Sigh) OK, just one personal story. It was thirty years ago. My parents both passed away while I was studying for my doctorate. I had no grandparents, aunts or uncles, or brothers or sisters. Just my wife, Ellen. Ellen was the only person in my life that ever actually listened to me, and wanted to know me. She helped me get through the grief of losing my parents. And she was the most gorgeous woman I ever saw. She was a perky blond with twinkling blue eyes. Full of life, and as sassy as they come. She brought so much joy into my life…. but I don't let myself think about that much any more. I will never know what she saw in me.

ME: What happened?

ARTHUR: I landed my first job as an adjunct instructor at the University. Ellen and I went together to all the faculty parties, and took long walks, and just enjoyed the privilege of being with each other. Christopher was conceived on the night of our first anniversary. I won't go into the details about the conception – but I don't think I have ever been happier than the night she told me we were expecting a baby.

We had a small house on the campus, and so we fixed up a nursery. Halfway through the pregnancy, we knew it was going to be a boy. And we loved just talking about what to name him. We settled on Christopher. We both had a lot of dreams about his future.

He was the most beautiful baby I have ever seen. He had Ellen's eyes, and when he smiled, his whole face lit up. And it made my face light up too.

ME: Your face lights up when you talk about him. So what happened?

ARTHUR: For six months, my life was about as perfect as I could ever hope for.

Then, I was at a faculty meeting one evening when I got a call from the hospital. Ellen and Christopher had been in the car, and a drunk crossed two lanes and smashed into them head on. The doctors did everything they could for them, but I lost both Ellen and Christopher that night.

ME: Oh, God. I'm so sorry.

ARTHUR: I did what you did. I walked the streets yelling at God. How could he let this happen? How could he be so cruel to let some drunk take out the only two people I ever loved? It was the only time in my life that I cried. But I had nobody to cry with.

ME: You believed in God at that time?

ARTHUR: Sort of. Ellen and I went to church together.

ME: Were the people in your church any help to you?

ARTHUR: One of them patted my hand and told me it was all God's will, even if I didn't understand it. Our priest gave me some mumbo jumbo about God moving in mysterious ways.

ME: That's not what you needed.

ARTHUR:

ME: I am so sorry that we failed you.

ARTHUR:

ME: Do you need a minute?

ARTHUR: I'm OK. Why did you say that *you* failed me?

ME: You were in a lot of pain. You probably still are. You need a lot more than platitudes from the people of my church. Platitudes just make the pain worse.

ARTHUR: That's all they had to give me. I don't know what I needed. Still don't.

ME: You're not over this, are you?

ARTHUR: I have my work, and my students.

ME: And that numbs the pain?

ARTHUR: I don't want to talk about this any more.

ME:

ARTHUR:

ME: Was that why you became an atheist?

ARTHUR: I don't want to talk about it. You have now succeeded in turning me into a complete stereotype.... The atheist who became an atheist because he was in pain and he didn't feel any love in his life.

ME: Sorry. I told you up front that I didn't know any atheists. So, you're the best I could come up with.

ARTHUR: I don't understand a God who can allow such evil to exist.

ME: I think it is OK to yell at God. It's like yelling at your own father when you can't make sense of things. Your father doesn't end the relationship if you yell at him when you're in pain. And I think God forgives us when we are human. He's the one who designed us with the ability to feel pain and react in anger.

ARTHUR: I don't know what my father would have done if I had yelled at him. I don't want to talk about this.

ME: OK, I don't know about you, but my brain seems to have stopped working anyhow. Why don't you come home with me to dinner. You can meet my wife.

ARTHUR: You're not going to hug me, are you?

ME: Promise.

ARTHUR: OK, but no hugs.

ME: No hugs.

ARTHUR: And I am still an atheist.

ME: I respect your beliefs. Or lack of beliefs.

ARTHUR: And I ... well, never mind.

ME: Where did we wind up our debate?

ARTHUR: Call it a tie. You gonna leave that martini there?

ME: Martinis are hard to carry around. The design of the glass is stupid.

ARTHUR: Hold on – it just occurred to me. Am I still a figment of your imagination?

ME: I don't know. You seem a lot more real to me now.

ARTHUR: Neither one of us should drive in this condition. So... lesh walk to your house, K?

ME: K.

Questions for Reflection and Discussion:

-Who are the people in my life carrying pain they don't want to talk about?

-How should I be living my faith with these people?

XIX. Stop and See

Denie, Denie
Measuring the marigolds…
Seems to me you'd stop and see
How beautiful they are!

You may recall this from the first chapter – the song I imagined my father singing to me. It led me to discover the first requirement for finding meaning through an informed faith: stop and see.

Since that time, I have unfortunately also discovered how hard this seemingly simple challenge has become. Like everything else, once I decided I wanted to stop and see, I also wanted to do it right now!   But that didn't happen. It's more like a lifetime of trying, mostly unsuccessfully.

The first part of "stop and see" is the hardest: stop!

The question that popped into my head was "stop what?" I had this fantasy that stopping so I could see better involved a simple act of my will. I just needed to stop whatever I was doing at the time – and clear my head. And then I would be able to see better. And that's the essence of an informed faith – just seeing better. Just discovering truths. Just clearing the clutter away – and there would be beauty right in front of me – waiting to be absorbed.

Right. It turns out that 95% of my life involves obligations that I cannot and should not stop if I am to live a responsible life. If I stop to reflect and contemplate something in the middle of my job - something not related to my job - then I am cheating the company of what they pay me to do. I cannot and should not neglect focusing on how to be effective in my fathering and husbanding in order to find hidden truths somewhere else. There are chores to do, housing to maintain, food to put on the table, conversations to have, listening when I find it a struggle… demands, demands, demands! Being a responsible person is a very important part of living an informed faith: turning my ideals (things I think are important) into lived values (things I am willing to make sacrifices for.) Living my faith is evidenced in what I do, not in what I think about. Yet what makes it an informed faith is that I do try to make myself stop and see… and think.

So, stop what? It's the 5% of my life that is not dominated by external obligations that is the only place where I have ethical opportunities to exert control. And I fill time that up with more distractions: mindless plopping in front of the TV watching Yankees games or March Madness or somebody wrestling a 200 pound catfish with bare hands; background music in the car or in an ear bud, Facebook, video games, texting, crossword puzzles, Sudoku, KenKen, golf, working out in the gym... the list is impressive. But, this is where I have control. I can continue with these self-imposed distractions, or I can choose to stop for a while at least, and make space in my life for reflection.

Reflection is a *value* for me – and it requires a conscious act of my will. What makes it a value (instead of an ideal) is precisely the fact that I choose it over all the other things I could be doing instead, and because I don't fall into it naturally. It would be simply an ideal if I stopped at just thinking it would be a good thing to do. It only becomes a value when I actually do it.

So, the fantasy version of "stop and see" is this: I turn the music off when I'm driving. Or I resist the temptation to turn on the computer or access my smart phone to see who is saying what. I walk away from the TV set. I put down the newspapers. I stop and see. And I reach a serenity and solitude that leads to deep thoughts and profound truths.

Right. It turns out that solitude all by itself didn't do anything good for me. It did not lead to peace and serenity and deep thoughts. When I stepped back from all the clutter in my life, what did I see? When I focused hard, listening to what was going inside my psyche, all I could see was residual tension. Reverberations. I could start to notice that my jaws were clenched, my muscles were knotted, my hands were like claws. I had been successfully coping so long that these physical signs of my tensions had become invisible to me, even though they were right there all along. These were not profound truths I was discovering. These were not even desirable states of being. These were the very things I was burying under all the self-inflicted distractions I chose for my 5% where I have the freedom to make choices.

So what do you do when you "stop and see," and you don't like what you see? Maybe the reverberations and tensions and clenched jaws were indeed important truths to discover. At least they were truths I had been ignoring. They were just not what I wanted to see. But, in fact, most discoveries of truths are not what I expect to see. What is "how beautiful they are" about reverberations and tensions and clenched jaws? Somehow, it seemed like I was just not doing something right.

I'm after good feelings. I want to feel tranquil, serene, enlightened, peaceful, in control, and energized. I don't want to feel tense, agitated, irritated, angry, fretful, resentful, and out of control. Truth or no truth, there is a certain way I want to feel in the process of finding meaning through an informed faith. Something was just not working.

But I remember something I heard on a Marriage Encounter Weekend many years ago: "feelings are neither right nor wrong – they just are!" They're not good or bad. They just are. They are truth. My choice is *not* whether to have them or not have them: my choice is whether to acknowledge them or try to bury them.

My feelings come from who I am and what I bring into a situation. My wife and I could both be looking at the same situation – like one of the grandkids doing something precocious – and feel completely different about it. She might feel delighted while I'm feeling irritated by the exact same event. It's not the situation that causes my feeling, it's me. It's what I bring along with me. It's all the other things that happened to me today, all the various interpretations I put on those things, all my programming since childhood, all my values and biases and distortions... it's who I am that generates my feeling reactions. But it's not right or wrong to feel a certain way. The morality is found in my actions (like growling at the precocious grandchild): in how I handle my feelings – not in the feelings themselves.

So, I "stop and see," and usually what I see is not what I want to see. But it is still truth. It is the beginning of discovery if I can allow myself to accept the reality of my own feelings. I need to give myself some quiet time to go the next step. What is driving me? Where is my internal engine taking me? How did I get to be the kind of person who reverberates so much that I have to "treat" it with pain-killers like social media and crossword puzzles? Where are my interpretations distorted? Why can't I see beauty right now?

Frankly, it is taking me a very long time to accept the truth, and the beauty, of my own feelings... especially the feelings I don't like having. But, this is a necessary step to finding meaning through an informed faith. Informed faith starts with digging inside, not living in my mind and thinking terrific thoughts about the nature of Jesus and what's wrong with my church, and who is God?

It takes more than just a few minutes to acknowledge and process my feelings. It has taken me many, many years – and I am still not there yet. But, I have come to believe that there is much gold to be mined if I start by being tuned into my own feelings. Only then can I begin to see how they are leaking out of me in ways I couldn't imagine... and affecting my non-verbal behavior, which adversely affects the people around me. And there is morality in the way I act on my feelings, even if I am not aware of the impact of my own behavior. Only by making a concerted effort to stay tuned into my own feelings can I start the process of discovering my own biases and distortions. Only then can I make progress on a journey to an informed faith – which encompasses both external truths and internal truths.

The deeper insights come later. It isn't just thinking through what Jesus said and what he meant that is important. Seeing all that with perfect clarity counts for nothing, unless I simply want to become an expert. For a person seeking *meaning* through an informed faith, the only thing that counts is how I am personally living those teachings.

And for me, that requires the discipline of reflection. I try to make time for reflection every day. And I write my reflections out in a notebook because it slows my brain down to the speed of my fingers – and that helps me to absorb things a little better... and let my insights actually sink in. For me, every reflection starts with a personal inventory: how am I feeling right now, and how might that bias/color/distort the way I am interpreting things. I find that this self awareness is important before I tackle the issues related to whatever is troubling me.

So, why is this chapter included in the section labeled "Evolving Faith?" I don't think of faith as a static thing – as if there are only so many truths included in my faith, and once I accept them, then I am a full-fledged member... my ticket is punched and I am saved. I think that informed faith means evolving faith... and the evolution comes from within... from my personal insights. Many times, those very insights are triggered by something I hear from the pulpit. But, there are questions about my God and my Church I will never be able to answer. The best questions have nothing to do with dogma.

And inevitably, the insights from my reflections tend to lead me back to the essence of an informed faith: religion is meaningless, Church is meaningless, God is meaningless... unless I continue to think about how I actually apply what I profess to believe in the way I treat the people in my life. It is my actions that bring meaning to my faith.

I can choose to "stop." That's the easier part. It takes a while to recognize both the truth and the beauty in what I "see" after I stop. Especially when it is not what I expected to see, or wanted to see.

Questions for Reflection and Discussion:

-What are some of the feelings I try hardest to ignore in myself?

-What are some ways I try to distract myself, and that keeps me from stopping and seeing?

XX. Fear of Gittin' Took

In the previous chapter, I mentioned that only by making a concerted effort to stay tuned into my own feelings can I start the process of discovering my own biases. Two key elements of an informed faith involve discovering my own biases, and then seeing more clearly how these biases distort my interpretations of the things I hear proclaimed. My biases are found in the acts of my internal spin doctor – and he is with me all my life. He may be right in the way he spins things, or he may be wrong. But he is always spinning, whether I want him to or not. My spin doctor can stand as a barrier to seeing objective truths for what they really are. Or in some cases, he might even help me to see the truth more clearly. If I am to find meaning through an informed faith, I just need to keep myself aware of what he is doing.

It is when I am oblivious to the effect my spin doctor has on the way I see and interpret the "truths" that are presented to me that I can have problems. That is when I settle for "my truth", and forget about my quest for "the truth."

Once I have mastered the challenges of staying tuned into my own feelings, acknowledging my inbred biases is an order of magnitude more important step in the quest to find an informed faith. It helps to know that the biases are always there, and everything I look at is distorted by them – even when they don't look at all distorted.

This piece is about my search to understand my own biases, and how they distort things.

I have been fixated on a couple of key questions about my religion in this book: Is Jesus really the Son of God? Does God actually care what I do? And, is there an afterlife? Most religious people are not hung up on these questions. For them, answering yes to these questions is simply an article of faith. So why am I so hung up on them? Could it be that these unanswerable questions are important to me because of my biases? If so, what biases could be at play here, and where did they come from? Is my inherent skepticism really a bias?

I am beginning to believe that it is. Here is what I have recently seen about myself relative to my inbred skepticism:

I hate to "git took." That's an expression my parents used to describe either getting talked into something I don't want to accept, or getting talked out of something I value – like my money. I have lived a great portion of my life on guard against gittin' took – probably because of some bad experiences in my earlier years, when I wasn't paying enough attention or asking myself the right questions.

One of these events happened when I was courting Dee. I took her to the Kentucky State Fair when we were about 18 years old. After paying admission, I had about six dollars left in my pocket to spend on her at the fair – which was sufficient in those days when the carnival rides cost a quarter, and the corn dogs were fifteen cents. At one point we were walking through the midway, trying to avoid the barkers who were determined to draw us in. But one of the games caught my eye. They gave you free practice rounds – and the prize was a huge teddy bear. Huge. As an 18-year old man of the world (I had actually been all the way to Miami), winning a huge teddy bear for my Dee would certainly fit the image of the man I wanted her to believe I was.

So, I tried a few practice rounds. The game was very simple. There was a softball hanging from a rope. All you had to do was hold the softball next to a milk bottle, then swing it back behind the bottle and have it knock over the bottle on the return swing. The game operator said it was easy, and he showed me how it was done. "See, just swing it like this, and it comes back and knocks over the bottle." Which it did. So, I tried it, and sure enough, I could knock over the bottle too. I tried it a second time and a third time, and I was very good at swinging the softball and knocking over the bottle. So, the operator invited me to try it for real. It only cost a dollar, and I would win the coveted teddy bear.

So, I gave him the dollar, swung the ball, and missed the bottle! OK, three out of four ain't bad, so I tried again. It cost me another dollar, and again I missed the bottle. Something was wrong. I tried again with a third dollar, and missed again.

Now I was getting red in the face. Not only was I not showing Dee what a sophisticated man of the world I was, but I had just frittered away half of what I was planning to spend on her at the fair. Dee was wise enough to gently take my arm and steer me away before I tried it again.

That experience troubled me for many years afterwards. How could I succeed so impressively when I was just practicing, and fail so dismally when it cost a dollar a try? It was about ten years later when it finally occurred to me that the operator placed the bottle in slightly different positions during the practice swings, and just moving the bottle an imperceptible quarter of an inch when there was a teddy bear at stake would cause the ball to miss the bottle on the return swing. I could finally see it: I got took!

A second event took place about a year after Dee and I were married. Dee was teaching school full time, and I was taking a full load of engineering courses at the University. I also worked full time as the night shift quality control inspector in a cookie factory. Together, Dee and I brought home about $350 per month after taxes. And every night after I got off work about midnight, I spent the next four hours working thermodynamic problems and studying for my other classes the next day. Even when I was sitting on the toilet, I usually had a fluid dynamics or LaPlace Transforms textbook open in front of me. And, every penny we made that wasn't paying for food, rent, or utility bills went into paying tuition.

One day, a magazine salesman knocked on the door with an incredible offer. For the low price of just five cents a day, we could subscribe to six magazines of our choice for the next five years. Pretty impressive. Before my job in the cookie factory, I worked as a page in the Louisville Free Public Library making ninety two cents per hour - and I loved leafing through magazines like *Mechanics Illustrated* and *The New Yorker* on my breaks. Any six magazines we wanted for five cents a day – what's not to like about that? So, we signed up. I never occurred to me that I didn't have the time to read six magazines each month.

After we signed the contract, a bill arrived for ninety dollars. What? What happened to five cents a day? I did the math, and discovered that five cents a day comes to ninety dollars over five years. I didn't remember the salesman mentioning that we had to pay it all up front. And now we were committed. We signed without reading the small print. We didn't even have enough money to buy cigarettes unless we could find a quarter between the cushions on the couch. Our total living expenses, which we were barely managing, came to just over $45/month plus whatever we spent on food that month. How in the hell were we going to be able to pay a bill for ninety dollars without either sitting out a semester or eating bread and water for two months? I got took again! The salesman didn't lie… he just presented the truth in a form that was misleading.

That's how I became a skeptic. To this day, I am instinctively cautious around carnival barkers and most sales people and, in fact, anyone who approaches me with an "incredible offer." Years after the magazine fiasco, a crusty old vice president at the high tech company I worked for had just returned from finishing school to knock off some of his rough edges. He was certainly a different person from before the finishing school. I noticed that he started responding to most of the things people told him by saying "incredible!" One time I asked him what he used to say instead of "incredible" before he went to finishing school. He answered "bullshit!"

So now, whenever I hear the words "incredible offer," I know what it really is. This crusty old VP became one of my heroes because of his skepticism. And I find myself saying "incredible" a little more than a normal person would.

But my fear of gittin' took goes back even further than these events. I was programmed to be skeptical and cautious even as a pre-teen. My parents grew up during the great depression, and they watched the banks fail and knew people who lost their life savings in the process. As a result, my Dad never had a checking account in all his life. He paid all the bills in cash. He worked for the Post Office, and when I was young, he received his pay in cash. Every Friday night, Mom and Dad budgeted their money by sitting at the kitchen table with about twelve mason jars in front of them... and they put a certain amount of money into each jar. One jar for the electric bill, one jar for groceries, one jar for tuition, etc. Then the jars all went into the cabinet above the refrigerator, and the money was there to pay the bills when they came due. When I was old enough, I remember being trusted enough to ride my bicycle to the drug store to pay utility bills. Mom emphasized again and again, "make sure you get a receipt, and put it in the jar." They didn't want to git took in case anybody questioned whether the bills were paid on time. And Mom and Dad never trusted anyone they didn't know well – and I too learned to be cautious by observing them.

Like all inbred biases, my fear of getting' took has upsides and downsides. One upside is this: I have become a very good money manager. My cautious approach keeps me from making too many mistakes. I have taught myself to ask some routine questions whenever I am faced with a proposition from another person. Those questions include: What is the probability that the other person is telling the truth? Is it the whole truth? And what's in it for them? I have learned to try to imagine myself in the shoes of the other person, and see the proposition from their vantage point. This often keeps me from making too many wrong assumptions.

So I don't get easily conned. Plus, I am a great negotiator. I recognized that I have power over those who want to separate me from my money as long as I am still holding onto the money... which gives me a lot of leverage in negotiations. I also don't give my trust easily to people, even when there is no money involved. I expect people to show me that they have integrity before I allow myself to trust them fully. And the result is that while I still get took from time to time, those are fairly rare events in my life. I have a sense of control most of the time.

One downside from having this skeptical bias is that it tends to define my relationships with others. I always stand back a little and scope things out before loosening up. And the impression many people have of me is that I am a bit stand-offish... at least at first, until we get to know each other. My inbred caution can be an impediment to my relationships with my adult children whenever one of them needs a bailout for some financial trouble they have gotten themselves into.

In these situations, the little voice in the back of my head keeps saying "Careful, don't git took." Fortunately, I am married to a woman with a beautiful, generous soul with an instinct to help whenever anyone needs help. And our two opposite instincts - my caution and her generosity - tend to complement each other. Over the years, I have become a little more like her, and she has become a little more like me. That doesn't make the little voice go away... but it gives me more willingness to override it.

Whenever some needy person approaches me on the street with their hand out, the voice pops up. This could be a scam. More often these days, I find I am able to ignore the voice by asking myself "so what if it is? I'm only out a couple of bucks, and that isn't going to ruin me." There is a reasonable chance that this person is in genuine need, so I am learning to selectively ignore the voice and shell out... at least more often than I used to. It is by being aware of my strong bias against "gittin' took," that I can start to allow myself to take the risk of gittin' took from time to time – and not worry about it.

So, I am starting to see this particularly bias a little more clearly, and selectively override it instead of always living on automatic pilot when it comes to my inbred skepticism.

That brings me back to my efforts to see more clearly how this bias against gittin' took plays out in my approach to religion. That bias is the thing that keeps me asking so damned many questions. I really do envy the people who can just accept religious truths as they are presented. They probably have different biases than mine – and sometimes their biases look more attractive to me. But a secret part of me also wonders if they are just being overly naïve.

The Christian ideal is to "be like little children," and I don't want to be like a little child when it comes to my faith. Little children "git took" all the time, mostly benevolently with stories about tooth fairies, Easter bunnies, and Santa Claus. Approaching Christianity "like a child" seems to put Jesus in the same company – and I don't want him to be a myth. I want him to be real. The myth of Santa Claus evolved from a real person called St. Nicholas, who actually existed and who started the practice of putting little gifts in the wooden shoes of children on Christmas Eve. St. Nicholas was living out his faith, not epitomizing the excesses of capitalism. I want to know the Jesus equivalent of St. Nicholas, not the Santa Claus version.

In my quest for meaning through an informed faith, the little "don't git took" voice keeps popping up. There clearly was a time when the hierarchy of my Church acted like carnival barkers or magazine salesmen – selling indulgences, threatening excommunication, torturing non-believers to convert them, etc. And that's not all in the past. Today, there certainly are a lot of TV evangelists around today who try to separate people from their money so that Jesus will love them more. Some Christians are pretty gullible.

But, as I told Arthur in a previous chapter, these things are not present in the Church I have experienced for myself. The priests, brothers, or nuns I have known have not been carnival barkers or salespeople trying to simply separate me from my money. I don't put my money in the basket because I think it will buy Jesus' love for me – I do it because I believe the institution of my parish is quite valuable and deserves to be supported. So, this is not where my biases show up in my approach to my faith.

My biases show up in my obsessions to understand the truth. For example, take the two central tenets at the core of Christianity: Jesus is the Son of God, and there is an afterlife we spend with God if we live a good life. Those two tenets have always troubled me because, as Arthur stated in a previous chapter, there is simply no way to prove either one of them. But more importantly, if the reality happens to be that there is no afterlife, and Jesus was simply a prophet, then there is no foundation to Christianity. All of Christianity is a fantasy that helps people cope with the unknowns and the difficulties in their lives. It would mean that Marx was right: religion is the opiate of the people.

That's not what I want Christianity to be. Why? Because I have just as much programming on the tenets of Christianity pounded into me as I have the fear of gittin' took. These two aspects of my programming are in considerable conflict with each other. That's not a comfortable place to be.

So, because I have tried hard to see how my fear of gittin' took colors and distorts the way I see and interpret things, I can now see how this bias manifests itself as simple compulsiveness to answer these two unanswerable questions. In an ideal world, I should be able to say "I see my biases at work here trying to prove something that is un-provable...So, get over it, self!" Move on. In my real world, that's easier said than done.

But I have made a bit of progress. While I can't seem to let go of these two questions, I have become a little more relaxed about not finding answers for them. In the process, I have become more aware that there are many layers to my skepticism.

Here's an example. Clearly, the New Testament proclaims both of these two fundamental tenets of Christianity to be true. But, as I have asked in the previous chapters: is the Bible true? Here's where the little spin doctor kicks in. A few years ago, I read all six of the Harry Potter books. J. K. Rawlings used her phenomenal imagination to create an entire alternative world at Hogwarts, and made it believable. Science fiction writers create all kinds of alternative universes, and draw us into them. I don't think creative people with vivid imaginations are a recent invention. I suspect there were a lot of them around when the Bible was being written too. I do not doubt that Jesus of Nazareth, unlike Harry Potter, was an actual historical character who had a lot of important things to say to us. But it could well be that the Gospel writers enhanced him quite a bit. It could also be true that the early church fathers created alternative universes called heaven and hell... and later purgatory, to facilitate the selling of indulgences... and that is what we are calling the inspired word of God these days. There is no doubt that the Gospels are inspired. But was it God who did the inspiring, or was it gifted people who were creatively solving problems for thousands of confused and frustrated followers of Jesus who needed some "truths" to hang onto? The second coming didn't happen when they expected it would, the world didn't end when they expected it would, and the nasty Romans were still making their lives miserable... as were the mainstream Jewish community who didn't believe Jesus was the Messiah. The followers of Jesus needed some hope to hang onto.

So, all these perspectives and questioning the truth in what is presented as truth is one layer of my bias at work. My bias actually frees me and burdens me at the same time. It frees me to ask serious questions - the way I wish I handled that magazine salesman. I am free to ask myself: What is the probability that the New Testament writers were telling the truth? Was it the whole truth? And what was in it for them? One answer is that they were just trying to give the people hope by telling the story of Jesus in a new and creative way. If that is true, then it is problematic for the foundation of Christianity. But there is as much probability that they were telling the whole truth. And billions of Christians over two millennia are not being conned.

The burden of my bias comes in the form of an obsession with a question I cannot answer for myself: Was Jesus the Son of God or wasn't he? Most clergy will say we can never know this for sure if we don't accept the New Testament as the total truth: so we just have to believe it.

But, I can't seem to let go of it. One of the practices I have developed as a result of this bias is standing in the shoes of the other person and asking "what's in it for them?" as a way to see the whole picture. I tried earlier to find more of the truth by standing in the shoes of the Gospel writers, but that didn't help very much in terms of the core question of whether or not Jesus is the Son of God. So, who else's shoes can I stand in here?

How about if I do a little thought experiment, and try to stand in God's shoes. (I do believe in God the creator, even if I'm not sure if he actually wears shoes.)

OK, so I am now God. And I am a benevolent God, because that's the kind of God I want to be. I have created this entity called the universe, and I probably overdid it a bit. I created a billion galaxies, each with a billion stars in them, and each star with a number of planets. Many of those planets (probably several hundred million of them), support intelligent life… people with whom I want to have a relationship. I want them to know me.

So, take Earth, for example. My people there have evolved a lot lately, and gotten to be pretty observant and intelligent. They have a beautiful sense of wonder for all that I created. They cannot yet imagine how big my creation is (billions of light years distance from one end to the other), and it will be a few more centuries before they even discover the full extent of my universe. How can they hope to have a relationship with a God that big? I might have intimidated them a bit.

I have two choices. I can turn myself into a much smaller God for a while, and take on the size of the Stay-Puft man, and walk around talking to each one of them telling them "I know you, I love you, and you are not just ant number 364,927 to me. You are my beloved son or daughter, and I want to have a relationship with you." But, if I did that, I would take away their freedom of choice. And it is important to me that they have a freedom to choose a relationship with me. If I imposed my presence on them, they wouldn't be free to choose me or not."

"So, that's not a good outcome. My second choice is to send them my Son. He will call me Abba, Daddy, and he will teach them how to talk to me. He will show them that I am not some cold, unapproachable God. He will show them that I really do care about each and every one of them, by name. He will teach

*them how to get along with each other in my name.
That's a good way to solve my problem."*

Hmmm. Thought experiment over. If God really is a benevolent God, then I could see how He might think this way. Of course, this is not a proof. But it is a possibility.

Does this thought experiment resolve my dilemma? No. The dilemma is un-resolvable. It just reassures me that I am not a complete idiot for wanting to believe in a benevolent God. It augments my belief that what Jesus had to say is worth listening to and guiding my life choices – whether He was the Son of God or not. It helps me to live with the uncertainty while trying to live out my faith.

So, I seem to be making a little progress in reconciling my two biases that are in conflict with each other: my fear of falling for something that is not true, and my desire to believe in the "truths" that Christianity teaches me.

So what about the other tenet – that there is an afterlife that we spend in God's presence for all eternity. That one is just as un-resolvable. It became especially troubling for me once I learned that in the several thousand years of history of the Hebrew nation prior to Jesus arrival, there were no thoughts or teachings about an afterlife. It was only about the time of Jesus that the Jewish people started to debate the point. And Jesus arrived right in the middle of the debate. He clearly believed in the afterlife. He said to the thief hanging on the cross next to him "you will be with me in Paradise" after his death.

This is one of the few times when Jesus sided with the Pharisees. It was the Sadducees that thought there was no afterlife, and they baited and taunted Jesus for his belief that there was one.

Now, referring back to the discussion of tenet number one, that Jesus is the Son of God, then this debate about an afterlife may not be all that important. If Jesus *was* the Son of God, and He believed in the afterlife... end of debate. Of course there is an afterlife. But, if Jesus was simply a gifted prophet and teacher, then the second tenet remains unresolved. He could have believed wrongly. The afterlife could have been invented and embellished by creative church people as a way of hanging onto their congregations and selling indulgences or, whatever. How do I go about resolving this dilemma. Whose shoes do I stand in to help me see things more clearly?

I can't think of any at the moment. So, the uncertainty remains a big deal for me.

The one thing that has helped ease my mind about this second dilemma is something I read many years ago. C. S. Lewis was wrestling with the same dilemma. His approach was to ask a very simple question: how are you going to bet?

Here are the two sides to the unknowable dilemma: either there is an afterlife (heaven) or there isn't. And the way I live my life either determines how I will spend the afterlife, or it doesn't.

The only choice I have, given the absence of any proof, is in how I live my life. That's the bet Lewis referred to. And here's how it plays out. If I try my best to be a good moral person, treating those around me with respect and dignity, and there actually is a heaven, then I will enjoy that afterlife. If there is no afterlife, then at least I have lived a good life to the best of my ability. If I choose instead to live a self-centered life, and am oblivious to the people I harm along the way, I may be successful and comfortable, but probably unsettled and miserable, and probably looking over my shoulder the whole time. If there is an afterlife, I will be excluded from enjoying eternity in God's presence. If there is no afterlife, then I wasted my life in self indulgence and probably hurt a lot of people in the process.

How am I going to bet? Trying to live the beatitudes creates a bit of heaven on earth, and the afterlife is a bonus. Living focused only on myself creates a bit of hell on earth, and the enjoyable version of the afterlife – if there is one – is denied me in the process. Maybe God has handed me the power to create heaven or hell right here and now... then live for all eternity with my choice. Or, if there is no afterlife, I have still created my own heaven or hell.

Looked at this way, it strikes me as a no-brainer. I can bet - with the way I live my life -that what I hope to be true actually is true. And if it isn't, I win anyhow.

My sister tells me I should not live in my head so much. Just accept what I have been taught, and life will be a lot less stressful. That is probably the hardest thing for me to do given that I have the burden of my bias. But, the same mind that harbors the bias is also capable of reasoning through the probabilities and possibilities, and it has brought me to a point where I can live with the uncertainties.

Besides, if I didn't have this particular bias, there would certainly be others that would take its place. As a society, we have a multitude of biases that inflict us, based on our individual life experiences. The people I previously labeled naïve have the opposite bias as me. They believe without questioning… and I am fairly certain that they also pay prices for their bias. Perhaps they "git took" more often, and get easily exploited by other people whose biases go something like "you don't get what you deserve, you get what you take." And I know a number of people who can just shrug in the face of uncertainties. Dealing with unknowns does not bother them in the least. Maybe their bias involves not trusting their own minds, and the price for that bias is that they live their lives in a mild state of oblivion.

Who knows? All I know is that I am the product of every experience that formed me. And I am a seeker of an informed faith. And, if truth be told, I kind of like being that way. If God really is the benevolent creator I believe Him to be, then it's probably all his fault anyhow. He is the one who inflicted me with this questioning mind. He might have even had a purpose in mind. And I suspect he doesn't want me to try to become somebody else in the process, and try to overrule what He created in me.

Questions for Reflection and Discussion:

-What are some of the biases in me that affect the way I approach faith?

-What are some of the prices I pay for my biases?

XXI. Informed Faith

One of my worries in writing this book is that people might conclude that I was advocating a brand new "Church of the Informed Faith" or something. Nothing could be further from the truth. I think people who are seeking a deeper meaning in their lives should start by staying right where they are – whether they are already part of a church, or have walked away from one, or have never been part of one. Informed faith is a lifelong process. You can't rush it. There is no recipe. There is no finish line. But, inevitably if you pursue a quest for an informed faith seriously, you are likely to see the need to make changes in the way you live.

Informed Faith is not a new religion, it is simply a means to an end – a means of achieving a greater sense of meaning and fulfillment despite all the uncertainties and irresolvable questions. For me, acknowledging the questions I had been reluctant to face was the hardest part. But that has often led me, over time, to have the courage to make changes in my life.

I wish I could tell you that my own journey has led me to a consistent sense of peace and serenity in my life. Sometimes I go around in circles, and feel dull and frustrated. Despite this, most of the time I feel a much stronger sense of fulfillment and wholeness just from knowing that I am at least trying to be honest with myself.

Here's a summary of my personal discoveries during my quest for meaning through an informed faith. It is unfortunate that I ended up with ten items. If anybody is tempted to make an association with the ten commandments, don't! These are simply things that work for me, and I invite you to see if they work for you.

1. Make the time to reflect. I must accept that my vision is distorted, and I often have blinders on. I must learn to give myself permission to "stop and see." If I "stop and see," my world will be neither confining or limiting.

2. If I am not living what I claim to believe in my relationships with the people I am closest to, then my faith and religion counts for nothing. Informed faith requires way more than discovering new insights and seeking objective truths. The hardest truths to discover are in my own behavior, and how that affects the people I live with.

3. Sometimes my faith doesn't give me a clue for what direction to take – especially when I want to make decisions quickly. Sometimes the only way to make moral decisions is to reflect, talk with the people affected, argue, let it cook, and wrestle with the issue for as long as it takes to feel peaceful about the

decision. Then, don't be afraid to take another path if that's where it leads me.

4. Righteousness left unchecked is a barrier to insight. Even in the best religious sense of the word, righteousness is usually thinly disguised bias, bigotry, and superior attitudes. It is a lifelong challenge to discover my own righteousness.

5. Sometimes, like with Jesus, faith is a matter of understanding the important principles behind the rules, and sometimes questioning how the rules are applied. An informed faith is built on questioning and searching. A person with an informed faith does not apply all teachings, church dogmas, laws, and proclamations universally or blindly, without thinking about the context. It remains important to listen carefully and with an open mind to what the hierarchy has to say; then reflect on it, research it, pray about it, spend time forming a conscience, and then act based on the best interpretation I can make.

6. A person seeking meaning though an informed faith will never find all the answers in this lifetime. Uncertainty is the dilemma of seeking an informed faith. Maybe that's all heaven is. Answers! And truth!

7. There is one God, but each of us sees Him not as He is, but as we are.

8. The overwhelming majority of people with religious vocations are sincere, dedicated, genuine, and worthy of our love and respect. Very few of them know that

they have our love and respect – perhaps because so few of us ever tell them.

9. For a Christian, the roots of an informed faith are based on a sincere effort to understand what Jesus actually taught, and how he behaved.

10. Life is too short to waste it on bad liturgies. I can't imagine that going through the motions for the sake of participating in a rite is pleasing to God. Good liturgies give me energy and peace, and sometimes insight. And they reinforce my values. In our world, where else am I challenged to throttle back my ego and compulsiveness. Not on TV, not in the newspapers, not in college, not from the politicians, not from Wall Street. If liturgies do what they are supposed to do, they affect how I live my life. What makes them good liturgies is not just what I get out of them, but equally important, what I bring to them in the form of an open heart and an open mind.

If you got this far in the book, I thank you for sticking with it. As I said in the beginning, I don't expect you to agree with everything I had to say. My gift to you is the questions. Your gift to yourself is what you do to find your own answers. My only hope is that I got you scratching your head from time to time, and perhaps seeing things from a slightly different perspective.

And I would love to hear from you.